The Personal Transformation Project

Books 1 - 6

P. Seymour

Table of Contents

A Note From Paula

What is the Personal Transformation Project?

I'm very excited to introduce you to this series called "The Personal Transformation Project".

As someone who is currently on a journey to lose 100+ lbs, I've become fascinated with the word "transformation" because I've seen the impact of what change can mean to a person's life.

AND I've seen the results of what can happen when you become so intentional and focused on specific goals. There is SO much power in this! I've seen it with myself but also with many of the amazing people I've had the privilege to come to know on the "How to Lose 100 Pounds" Facebook page. (You can find out more about this at the end of the book if weight loss is something that interests you too.)

What would it mean to YOUR life to go through a process of transformation?

Online I find this definition for the word transformation:
A marked change, as in appearance or character, usually for the better. (thefreedictionary.com)

I also think of the word "metamorphosis" when I think about transformation and change and of course this makes me think about the lowly caterpillar becoming a beautiful butterfly and the ugly duckling becoming the most beautiful of swans.

BUT change is not only about outward appearance and the things that others can notice easily when they come in contact with us. (These might be things like weight loss, physical "toys" that are a result of making more money or an increased awareness of emotional connections with others - just to name a few examples.)

Change can also (and maybe firstly) involve change on the inside - how one feels and thinks...then translated into how someone behaves in the world.

Part 1 of the series - How to Feel Awesome!

I'm dividing the series further into parts and the first part is what I consider a foundation of sorts - for most people this has to do with how we feel.

I'm excited for you and all the possibilities that your future holds!

Each individual book is meant to be a blueprint to help you recognize ways that you can find more success and happiness in your day-to-day living. I VERY much appreciate your reviews and comments as I love to put a name to those who are creating a healthy and happy life. I would love to be your biggest cheerleader if you'll let me.

To YOUR success,

Paula

Visit the link below to download my FREE gift to you (and be notified of new titles within the series).

http://ABiggerPlan.com

Please also join us on FaceBook:

The Personal Transformation Project
http://www.facebook.com/personaltransformationproject

How to Be Happier: A Blueprint for Creating More Joy in Your Life

What is Happiness?

Happiness is perhaps one of the things people say they want most in their lives. There have been several movies written around the concept of happiness. Poets, scholars, Jesus and even Albert Einstein have all written about happiness. One of the most famous lines about happiness appears in the United States Declaration of Independence, it reads "Life, Liberty and the pursuit of Happiness."

Sometimes just watching a movie or an uplifting human interest story can bring a smile and feeling of happiness to your heart. The smile of child, the antics of your cat or dog, winning the lottery or a dinner for two from your church raffle can all instill a feeling of sincere happiness. Some of these things create temporary feelings and others are long lasting.

So what exactly is happiness?

Well that depends on who you ask, and that's because outside of the definition you find in your dictionary, everyone has a different idea of what happiness means to them. For some, happiness is the love of family and friends and for others it may be having a certain amount of money. Having a relationship with God is a big part of the happiness equation for me.

There is however one aspect of happiness that is true in every case no matter who you are. Happiness is a state of being. True happiness creates an emotional response that is positive and can cause a real physical reaction called endorphins to be released throughout your system. When you're happy your brain releases these "feel good" endorphins. (More on that later)

One thing is for sure…happiness is something we all want as much as we can handle.

In this guide I'll give you some ways to be happier and get a little more out of your life at the same time.

Before you can enjoy more happiness, you need to take a little happiness inventory.

How Happy Are You? Happiness F.A.Q.'s

Let's talk about your happiness and give you a way to determine your level of happiness. Now this is not a scientific test by any means. It is simply a set of questions you can ask yourself to help you decide just how happy you are or aren't.

I like to call them the F.A.Q.'s of Happiness. Take a piece of paper and write the answers to the following questions before reading the rest of this section. No cheating. Take your time and be honest with your answers.

- What's going on in your life right now in terms of how you're living your life?
- When was the last thing, event or person that made you happy and what was it about it that made you happy?
- What is your definition of the word happiness?
- What makes you happy?

Remember, sit down and answer these questions before you continue on to the rest of this section.

Welcome Back!

So how did that go? Now take a look at your answers as they will be the best indicators of just how happy you really are right now. Since everyone is different there are no right or wrong answers, however, your answers can reveal a lot about how you're feeling about your life right now and whether or not you're happy.

Let's take a look at each one.

What's going on in your life right now in terms of how you're living your life?

If your answers are more about what's wrong in your life than what's right then that's an indication you're not as happy as you could be. Whatever level of happiness you do have may be something you experience only when something special happens to you and may only last as long as the moment or event. If, on the other hand, your answer was more focused on the positives in your life, your overall happiness level is probably better than the average person.

When was the last thing, event or person that made you happy and what was it about it that made you happy?

This one is pretty easy and if you had to spend an extended amount of time trying to remember you're happiness level is about average. Most people associate happiness with events or situations so it's not unusual if you have to search your memory.

What is your definition of the word happiness?

Again, there's no right or wrong answer, but pay close attention to how you answered this question. The answer you came up with says a lot about what you believe happiness is and what you believe makes you happy in your life. If you go back and read it out loud and you start to feel even a little uncomfortable about your answer it could mean either you're not being honest with yourself or you left something important to you out of your answer.

What makes you happy?

You might feel that whatever makes you happy would also be the same as your definition of happiness. I would be willing to bet your answer to this question is different from your definition. That is most likely because we have all been conditioned to think happiness is defined in a certain way. When we go deeper and ask ourselves what really makes us happy as individuals, the answers change dramatically.

This exercise is meant to get you to really think about and reflect on the concept of happiness. Hopefully by now your thoughts about happiness go a lot deeper than you may have realized. Basically I think we can all use a boost to our happiness IQ, but is happiness something that can be learned? You might be surprised at the answer. I'll answer that in the next section.

Can Happiness Be Learned?

I don't know if you can really get a degree in happiness but it would be pretty cool if you could don't you think? Of course that would mean that happiness is something you can learn to be. I believe happiness can be learned because it is an emotion and state of mind just like anger, negativity, envy, kindness, joy and a long list of others. When we're children we develop personality traits of who we will become as adults. For example, when you're young you can learn to be selfish or giving and depending on which one you become it can become a part of who you are as a person.

You probably know someone in your life…either in your family, a friend or an acquaintance at work who always seems to be happy all the time. Do they have a special happy gene or have they learned over time to be happy? In my opinion, happiness is a learned habit. If you grow up around happy individuals you will pick up on the habits of these individuals and eventually they become natural to you. Just as if you grew up around someone who was constantly negative all the time, you will be more likely to develop the same way of thinking or acting because of your exposure to this negativity. Eventually that negative mindset can become a habit if you are not conscious of it.

So how can you learn to be a happier person?

It's not a difficult thing to do, but just like learning anything for the first time, it's going to take commitment and action on your part. I can give you some useful simple strategies to change your current mindset but it's going to be up to you to follow through.

Are you up for the challenge? Good!

Let's go!

Strategies For Becoming a Happier Person

You Can Be Happier Starting Right Now

Are there different things you can do to be a naturally happier person? You bet there are! I've put together some easy things you can do right away to raise your happiness IQ and get more joy out of your life.

I've created simple but powerful happiness strategies you can use in your everyday life. No special tools are required…just you and your promise to choose a strategy that works best for you and stick with it.

How Will You Know If You're Happier?

Trust me, you'll know! When you find yourself feeling more optimistic about things, when you begin to notice you have a natural ability to adjust your mindset when things don't go according to plan in a calmer manner and when things that used to get on your last nerve don't anymore, that's when you'll know your happiness IQ has gone up significantly.

You will learn:

- How to develop a spiritual mindset that will not only make you happier but can change your life in amazing ways if you are open to it!

- How to put Hollywood to work to help you become happier.

- How to use smiling and laughter to make yourself happier each day.

- How gratitude can help you lead a happier life.

- How eliminating this one food additive could increase your happiness.

- How exercise can open up the happiness flood gates!

- Avoid this habit and you'll be feeling happier within 24 hours guaranteed!

- How meditation and a quietness of mind can help you be calmer, more grounded and happier.

- How to become happier by helping others and getting out of your own comfort zone (or pity party!)

- How having goals and a vision for bigger things in your life will naturally help you to feel happier with your life now.

You can try one or all of the strategies until you find something that works for you. If you enjoy them all, great! Some are better for lifting your mood if you've had a bad day but you're otherwise a naturally happy person. Others are best for forming new habits that lead to changing your mindset for being happier gradually over time.

The first strategy is about connecting on a spiritual level to something (someone) bigger than yourself. As a Christian, this is in my opinion a long term solution to leading a life full of happiness. Please note that this next section may be relevant to you regardless of your faith or spiritual beliefs, so please read on or skip it if you don't find it useful to your own life.

Strategy 1: Find Happiness Connecting To The Spiritual

As a Christian, I'm particularly drawn to the word transformation because I know the transformative power of what it means to know Christ.

Do not conform to the pattern of this world, but be transformed by the renewing of your mind. Then you will be able to test and approve what God's will is—his good, pleasing and perfect will. ~ Romans 12:2 (NIV)

BUT WAIT - If you are not a Christian I must say that I completely respect you and you will not be bombarded with scripture throughout this book. I may use my own personal examples to illustrate something when talking about the area of spirituality, but you will find your own way and what that journey is for you.

When you can connect to a source greater than yourself, you won't have to look for happiness, it will come from within. Your mind quiets and you don't worry about the small stuff anymore because there is no room in your heart, your mind or your soul for anything but the peace, love and all the happiness you can stand! Connecting on a spiritual level doesn't require you to be special or look a certain way. It doesn't require you be anything more than who you are right now.

What it does require is your heart and a genuine desire to connect to a higher being that lives within each and every one of us. For me this has everything to do with my Christian faith and for you this journey may mean something different. I do see this spiritual element as vital to one's level of "true happiness".

How Do You Connect On A Spiritual Level?

"Ask and you shall receive."

I believe that if you determine to quiet your body and mind for a period of time, being intentional about connecting to something bigger than yourself, you will begin to find an inner peace (and maybe even answers to a lot of questions) that can support and guide you on your journey to happiness and joy.

For me this quiet time involves reading the bible and prayer.

Don't worry if you are not used to praying - there is no magical formula to it - mostly it involves "being real" about your feeling and the questions you might be seeking. If you are comfortable praying to God, try to think of it as if you are speaking to a good friend.

The section on meditation also covers a strategy that can help guide you to a deeper place spiritually. If you are not comfortable with the idea of prayer, meditation might be a very good fit for you.

Go Where Your Spirit Can Connect!

Attending church or other places of worship is the ideal setting to allow yourself to connect to the spiritual. In addition to attending worship services consider getting involved with other members in fellowship. When you surround yourself with like-minded individuals your spirit will feel comforted and happier in every area of your life!

Other Activities That Help You Stay Connected Spiritually

Reading books like the Bible (and other spiritual titles), attending Bible study and going to relevant seminars or retreats are all examples of things one can do to can help you stay strong in your faith and lead a happy life.

Strategy 2: Hooray For Hollywood!

The Pursuit of Happyness!

No that's not a misprint. It is the way it was spelled for the release of a box office hit film starring Will Smith. The movie was based on the true story of Chris Gardner who went from being homeless to becoming a stockbroker and finally forming his own multi-million dollar brokerage firm. Now that's a theme that makes you feel happy and brings a smile to your face when you watch. Watching movies that make you laugh, smile and leave you feeling good can give you a shot of virtual happiness to get you out of the dumps.

Look for movies that are family friendly so that you can include the entire family and enjoy watching them together. If your overall level of happiness is a bit above average but you do get down from time to time, a good movie and your favorite snack could be all you need to get back on the happiness track! Plus, let's not forget about television shows.

Here's a list of a few movies that have "feel good themes" that can lift your spirits.

Forrest Gump
The Pursuit of Happyness
Happy Feet
The Parent Trap
Finding Nemo
Shrek
Toy Story
The Sisterhood of The Traveling Pants

You get the idea!

Television

Enjoy some goofy fun from old television shows like I Love Lucy or look for reruns of some of your favorite shows that always made you laugh.

You can create your own special collection of movies and television shows that make you feel good when you need it. Curl up in front of the TV and enjoy!

Strategy 3: Smile You'll Feel Better!

In the first section of this guide I mentioned how just smiling and laughter can release what are called "feel good endorphins" into your system.

How Laughter Makes You Feel Happier

Real laughter that begins because of something someone says or does can be contagious and it is this kind of laughter that causes your brain to release those feel good endorphins into your system. That results in you feeling good and happy. Fake laughter or laughter that is associated with something negative does not release the same endorphins.

A study by Dr. Robin Dunbar a psychologist at Oxford found that another benefit to laughter is the ability to increase our resistance to pain.

Why this happens is still a bit of a mystery, but clearly laughter is great for helping you to lead a happier life.

Laughing Strategies

Starting today, find things to do that make you laugh. If you're into stand up comedy, get some DVDs of your favorite comics and hit play. Is there something your kids do that cracks you up every time? Do you have pets? They can be a major source of laughter because they have personalities that can make them a real hoot to watch! Got any home videos from the 80's?

Think About Things That Make You Happy

Just by thinking about things from your past that make you laugh is another way to get yourself feeling good and happy. Recalling fun times with family and friends is another sure way to get those endorphins flowing.

So your assignment is to find things to do that literally make you fall down laughing! Make it a regular thing to do each day at least once. Gradually you'll find yourself looking for more and more ways to laugh because of the way it makes you feel.

Strategy 4: Gratitude Works Every Time!

The act of saying thank you to someone can make you feel better when it's for a gift that you've received or a compliment someone pays you, but it can also create a new level of happiness in your life that can last a lifetime!

The strategy behind gratitude is simple and powerful. Instead of being thankful only when something good happens to you, practice being thankful for everything in your life every single day. There are so many things to be grateful for that I guarantee you will never run out of something to say thank you about.

Here are a few things to be thankful for in your life.

Family
Without the love of your family where would you be?

Good health
If you get up every day and you're in good health, that is something to be thankful for as there are many on this earth who would give almost anything to have what you have.

Home
Millions of people live their lives on cold streets 24 hours a day. Your home may not be perfect but you can feel grateful you have a roof over your head.

Your job
The economy has created a worldwide crisis where unemployment is the highest it's been in decades. Your current job may not be perfect but you should give thanks you have gainful employment.

Vision
We don't think much about saying thank you for things we are so used to having until it's gone. Be thankful for the ability to see the sun, the smiles of your loved ones, your reflection in a mirror and other beautiful things that surround you each day.

That's just a very small sample of everyday things that you can say thank you for. Make it a habit of saying thank you for different things in your life and soon you'll notice how much happier you'll begin to feel every day without even thinking about it!

Can you think of some more things to be thankful for? Some people even like to write things down in what could be a called a gratitude journal.

The key is to stay consistent, it takes time to build your new happiness habit but if you stay the course I promise you'll love the new you!

Strategy 5: Cut This From Your Diet & Be Happier

Decrease the amount of sugar in your diet and not only will your heart and other organs be happier but so will you! Sugar tastes good but unfortunately it's one of the worst additives added to food for a number of reasons. Too much refined sugar and foods that act like sugar in your body contributes to weight gain, heart disease, kidney disease, high blood pressure, blocked arteries, tooth decay and it can contribute to major complications if you have diabetes.

Read that last sentence again out loud.

Now how do feel?

Nothing about that sentence makes you feel happier does it? Obviously all of those maladies are nothing to feel good about, but another thing you may not be aware of is the effect sugar has on mood. Studies show that those diagnosed with ADHD have an increase in hyperactivity when sugar is consumed in excess. Although sugar can give you an initial "feel good high" it is short lived and you end up crashing which can leave you feeling depressed. There are also studies that suggest avoiding sugar before engaging in activities where you have to work out logistics, design something or engage in writing or something creative, will help you to think and focus more clearly.

So imagine over time that you decrease the amount of sugar and other related foods in your diet. You will gradually feel happier for several different reasons.

You will:

- Look and feel better because you will lose weight and improve your health overall. Those are definite reasons to feel happier!

- Function better because your thinking won't be clouded by the effects of sugar.

- Enjoy higher energy levels because your body won't be run down due to having to work overtime to process all of that sugar.

Can you see how your level of happiness can increase just from making this small change?

By the way here are some foods that you might want to consider cutting back on if you decide to decrease sugar in your life.

Refined white sugar
White flour
White rice
White bread

Strategy 6: Exercise For Health & Happiness

Exercise is not only good for your health but it's also an excellent way to help you be happier! There have been several studies that show those who exercise regularly feel happier about themselves and their lives and have a lower rate of depression compared to those who don't exercise.

It's because of those "feel good endorphins" I mentioned before. When you exercise your brain floods your system with endorphins. These endorphins are also able to block pain so you can work out harder.

In addition to feeling good exercise has been known to:

- Increase your mood
- Decrease anxiety
- Boost your self confidence
- Give you a better night of sleep

All of the above combined automatically equals a happier you!

So if you're not exercising, it's time to get moving! Let the power of exercise give you a better body, healthier outlook and many more days of happiness!

Strategy 7: Put Yourself On A Mental Diet!

Take A Break From Information Overload

This strategy may be difficult for you depending on your lifestyle. If you're a news junkie or if you like watching a lot of television this strategy can be really challenging. You can increase your happiness by tuning out all the negative media that we're bombarded with every single day.

How News, Images And Other Content Can Rob You Of Your Happiness

In 1999 Princeton University released a study on the effects violence had on children. The study concluded that by the time a teenager reached the age of 18, they witnessed 16,000 simulated murders and 200,000 acts of violence thanks to television, video games, the Internet and movies. That study was more than a decade ago. Can you imagine what those numbers look like today? Talk about taking all the joy and happiness out of life!

Can you see how too much negative media and violent images can affect how you perceive your environment and your life in general?

It may be tough in the beginning but I can guarantee that your mood and overall happiness level will improve in as little as 24 hours if you tune out. That means avoiding television shows that feature murders and other activities that are devoid of anything happy. Make an effort to focus on things that are known to increase your happiness, such as exercise as an example.

I'm not saying that you should never watch anything ever again. I'm saying that you might want to be more aware of what you're choosing to invite into your consciousness and everyday life.

Find other activities, read books that educate, enlighten and give you something to feel good about in your life. Also, try some of the other strategies I've included and see how much better you feel. Challenge yourself to go for longer and longer periods without watching so much negative media. The longer you can tune out the better your experience will be over time. You'll find out that you probably aren't missing out on much and you may decide to make tuning out a regular part of your life.

Strategy 8: Meditation

If you're a Christian like me, than you may already be aware of how peaceful and happier life is when you meditate on the word of God. Reading devotional scripture each morning creates a natural sense of well-being, I feel happier almost instantly and this carries me throughout my day so I can focus on getting things done.

Breathing Meditation

Meditation is something that can certainly be beneficial, regardless if you practice a specific faith or not. You can also try a simple meditation that only requires you to focus on your breathing.

Tools

A timer set to 15 minutes

1. Find a comfortable place that is quiet where you won't be disturbed for 15 minutes.

2. You can perform this meditation lying down or sitting comfortably in a chair.

3. Inhale slowly and deeply filling your lungs completely with air. Hold for just a second or two and then slowly exhale.

4. Repeat this twice. You should be feeling more relaxed.

5. Next, take the index finger of your right hand and gently close the nostril on the right side of your nose and inhale through your left nostril.

6. Then place your index finger of your left hand over your left nostril and exhale through your right nostril.

7. Try to focus your attention on your breath. To keep your mind from wandering you can count each breath as you inhale and again when you exhale.

Continue this inhale and exhale, alternately closing your nostrils for 15 minutes. When you have completed the meditation session you will feel relaxed and you will be in a much happier state of mind due to this increased relaxed state of being.

Strategy 9: Volunteering

Volunteering is an amazing way to be happier. Just the act of giving up your time to be of service to others (usually perfect strangers) is a feeling that you can't really describe to someone. You have to experience it for yourself.

Why Volunteering Has Such A Positive Effect

When you can give unconditional support and love to someone who may not have family to take care of them, you'll probably see a level of gratitude on their face that can fill your heart and your spirit! I also think that when you are able to see firsthand how much someone appreciates your time and kindness, you can't help but smile and feel a lot happier. It is a form of happiness that never leaves you.

There are no shortage of organizations that are always looking for volunteers.

1. Non-profit organizations, especially in small towns where resources are limited, rely heavily on volunteers to spend a few hours a week visiting elderly dementia patients to give family members much needed respite assistance. You can contact social services agencies and non-profits in your area and ask about volunteering.

2. Nursing homes and assisted living centers are always looking for volunteers to visit elderly patients to brighten their day just talking, watching television, playing cards or shopping trips.

3. Youth agencies need volunteers to encourage teenagers to dream big. They are often from poor neighborhoods and need tutoring in reading and mathematics.

4. There are many local organizations or homeless shelters that can use volunteers to help serve meals to those who are less fortunate.

Animals

If you're an animal lover, especially of dogs and cats, there are a number of shelter and rescues that are understaffed with shrinking budgets in need of volunteers. Contact local shelters in your area and ask about lending a hand.

Strategy 10: Setting Goals

When you take the time to sit down and set goals, you are creating a blueprint of how you wish your life to be. If you sit down with the mindset that you can dream as big as you can handle, that's a lot of fun! It will make you feel happier just filling in all the details of the changes you will be looking forward to making in your life. That's just the beginning! When you set your goals and then go about taking the appropriate action to realize them…that's when you really begin to experience an intense feeling of happiness.

In my book "Resolutions in the New Year…or Any Time: How to Make a Plan for Transformation", I cover in detail how to go about setting and reaching your goals.

Here are a few tips you can use to begin setting your goals.

1. Sit down and get a clear idea of what it is you want to change, have, do or become in your life.

2. Next, write down your goals in as much detail as possible including the steps you'll need to take.

3. Begin working on your goals one by one, taking action step-by-step until you finally reach your goal.

Just the act of writing your goals down and then actively focusing on getting each task done will make you feel a lot happier about where you're headed in life. The more you accomplish goal wise, the happier and more confident you become as you take on bigger goals throughout the rest of your life.

A Note About Depression

Thinking Happy Thoughts Is Not A Cure For Clinical Depression

If you're feeling severely depressed you may be suffering from depression and you should seek the help of a professional right away.

Symptoms of Depression

There are several symptoms that are associated with various forms of depression.

- Insomnia
- Loss of interest in everyday activities or other things you used to have passion for.
- Decrease in energy and constant fatigue
- Feeling worthless
- Sad
- Thoughts of suicide
- Loss of appetite, overeating, digestive problems and other forms of physical pain

Depression is a very real disorder that can be treated. If you feel your sadness or depression is more than what would be considered normal or if you're having thoughts of suicide you need to get help immediately.

If you are diagnosed with depression, it can be treated with medications like anti-depressants, anti-anxiety and stimulants. Psychotherapy is also used to help anyone diagnosed with depression with coping skills to improve their quality of life.

One Last Word About Happiness

Developing a state of happiness takes time and can become as natural as smiling, but it's also important to keep in mind that we are all human. You're going to have good days and days that will challenge your new happy state of mind.

If you are always focused on becoming happier using the strategies I've included you will gradually reach a point where your ability to bounce back happens faster and you'll be less likely to let yourself revert back to your old habits.

You Have A Choice

If you are not suffering from a medical condition that would keep you from enjoying a normal more happier life, you have a choice to make right now. You can choose to make happiness a brand new habit in your life, or you can choose to not to do anything at all. If you do decide to see what happens when you focus on developing and improving your happiness IQ, get ready to experience everything in your life from a wonderful and fulfilling new point of view!

How to Be Motivated: A Blueprint for Increasing Your Motivation

Understanding What Motivation Is

Motivation is one of the most important things you need when it comes to having more of what you want in your life. You're reading this book because for whatever reason you believe you're not motivated to do whatever it is you want to do. Here's the thing...you're already motivated to do certain things in your life. I think it's impossible to not be motivated about anything, instead it's the kind of motivation you have that makes the difference in the results you're having or not having in your life. Motivation can be positively or negatively influenced but it's always present in some form.

For instance, when you're thirsty you become motivated to get up and go where you know there is a beverage of some sort to quench your thirst. Motivation is the action you take to help you get a desired result.

Let's take a look at some different kinds of motivation.

Motivated By The End Result

Jane has been working for the same company for 10 years. It's not the career she wanted but she took the job anyway. She's got great benefits and likes the people she works with. When she wakes up every morning to go to work, there is something that motivates her to do this same ritual day after day after day even though it's not quite what she envisioned 10 years ago. Why? What's the motivation? It may be that her job pays well and she can pay her bills so it's better than not being employed. The motivation in this scenario isn't that she goes to work each day because she loves what she does for a living. It's for financial security.

If Jane had spent the last 10 years working in the career she dreamed of and actually loved her job but made less money than she makes now, do you think she would still be motivated to get up each morning and go to work?

Most likely the answer would be yes even though her motivation for doing so would be different. The end result of working in a career she truly loves would be her motivation.

Motivation For Some Only Comes As A Way To Avoid Some Consequence

Kirk goes for a routine check up and his doctor tells him he's a borderline diabetic. Right then and there he decides to cut back on his intake of sugar and lay off the sweets. What's the motivation in this example? Is it to lead a healthier lifestyle or is it fear? If Kirk wasn't diagnosed a borderline diabetic, do you think he would still be motivated to cut back on his sugar intake? Who knows? He may be the kind of person who has to have something happen before he is motivated to take additional action in his life. Maybe gaining an extra 20 lbs may be the motivation he needs to change his eating habits. Otherwise if there's no risk or consequence involved, in this case to his health, then he may be motivated to continue eating lots of sweets.

Motivation Isn't Always Logical

If you shop for a car that is more expensive than you can afford comfortably but you choose to buy it anyway, you are motivated in some way to go ahead in spite of it being too pricey. What's the motivation? Is it because it's your dream car and you just have to have it or maybe you want to be able to impress your friends and family? Although the motivation for buying the car isn't a good idea from a financial perspective, it's not the money or lack thereof that motivates you to buy the car. In this example the motivation is the feeling you'll have driving around in that brand new car and the attention you're likely to get from it as well.

Motivation Negatively Focused

You and another are both up for a promotion that each of you is equally qualified for but there is only one position available. You are motivated to perform your work duties at the highest level in hopes of getting the new job. Your competition is also motivated but in a different way. He or she decides to work hard at making you look bad to management, hoping to eliminate you from the running so the job will be theirs.

Both of you are motivated, but only one is motivated negatively.

Motivation Positively Focused

Let's say you've decided you want to quit your job and start your own business. Instead of giving two weeks notice, you sit down and write out a detailed plan about your business. You're almost ready to take the plunge when you realize after doing some number crunching, you're going to need a hefty cash reserve to live off of to pay bills and such until you're business catches on. After giving it lots of thought you decide to keep your job and start your business part-time. You end up working long 18 hour days juggling your regular 9 to 5 and your new business venture. You start your day at 5 am and often you don't get to bed until midnight, but you're determined to do what's necessary and make sacrifices like eating out less and holding on to your old car instead of buying a brand new one to save money.

What's the motivation? Well it's pretty obvious that your motivation is the freedom to work for yourself and leave the 9 to 5 rat race behind. You want to be able to decide who, when and how much you will earn…everything to do with your own work life. You are motivated to put in the extra work to achieve your dream. The results are a positively charged mindset of motivation to do what you must do to be successful.

You Can Learn To Be Motivated In A Way That Is Constructive And Positive

So you see motivation exists in everything you do. What's important is to recognize exactly what your motives are and whether or not you have the right kind of energy behind your motivation to achieve whatever it is you want in your life. Positive motivation is the key to enjoying more and achieving your goals. The reason is just as simple. When you go about your life doing things with a mindset focused on being positive, honest, thankful and setting your standards higher, the results you will experience will be better than you could have ever dreamed of. Going the opposite route may not mean you will automatically fail, but in the end I guarantee something else you're passionate about in your life will.

So, can you learn how to be motivated in a more positive way? I believe you can! Let's move on to the next section "Positive Motivation Can Be Learned" and see how.

Positive Motivation Can Be Learned

Increasing your motivation the right way is something I believe anyone can learn. It is simply a new habit you need to create in your life. If you're like most people, when you think of the word habit, you tend to first think of "bad habits" as if having a habit of doing anything must be bad. A habit in itself can be good or bad.

So you simply need to get into the good habit of being positively motivated more of the time in your life. Now if you happen to find it difficult to be positive about pretty much everything, I suggest reading my book "How to Be Positive" before you try to develop positive motivation.

Like any other habit, you need to do something over and over again until it becomes routine for you. Here's an example...if you decided to lose 100lbs like I did, you would have to develop some new habits in order to increase your chances of being successful right? This would include things like eating a healthier diet that promotes weight loss and exercising regularly. If those are habits you don't have, you have to commit to doing them every day until they become a natural way of doing things for you. They then become so ingrained in your lifestyle that eating right and working out eventually become new habits.

So when you're working on being more motivated, it's going to require you to be a lot more aware of your thoughts and the choices you're making when setting goals and other targets in your life. It all starts with you. There's no magic formula that will make you instantly more motivated, but there are specific steps you can take that will help you become more motivated gradually over time.

The Blueprint For Increasing Your Motivation

In the next sections you'll learn steps you can take to increase your motivation.

Here's what you can expect:

- Motivation - **Getting A Clear Picture**: Before you can be inspired or motivated to do something, you have to have a clear view of what it is you want in your life. This section will help you do that.

- Motivation - **Get It In Writing**: Writing down your goals will help you get motivated, in this section I'll give you some easy tips on how to get your goals down on paper.

- **Make YOUR List**: You can have any number of goals in your life, but you also need to know what gets you so motivated that not trying is not an option. The best way to do that is to make a list. I'll give you some ideas on where to look for the things that can move you to take action.

- **Strategies**: Finally, I've put together several strategies you can take advantage of to help you increase motivation in your life.

Motivation - Getting A Clear Picture

In order to find the motivation you need to achieve something you have to set clear goals about what you want. Getting a clear picture means sitting down and giving your goals and dreams a new level of importance. You may have a general idea about what you want in your life but until you create a solid vision of what that is, you'll waste a lot of time going from day to day talking about what you want but never actually taking the proper action to see it through.

Tools You Need

1. Collect your dreams and get ready to work!
2. Find a quiet spot where you won't be disturbed.
3. Voice recorder (mp3 recorder, your computer etc)

Recording yourself talking about what you want can reveal a lot more about yourself than writing everything down initially. That's because when you have to write so much detail, it's easier to get mentally blocked. Before you know it, you can get distracted and suddenly find yourself doodling silly pictures instead of your goals. (Been there done that!) I'm not saying you shouldn't write things down, in fact in the next section that's exactly what you'll be doing. Recording yourself allows you to let your imagination and thoughts flow.

Talk To Your Friend

Before you begin recording pretend that you're having a conversation with a trusted friend about what you want in your life. This imaginary friend is supportive and never lets you down. For me the best friend I could ever have is God, so I would talk openly and freely to Him. If that works for you, great! If not, go with the imaginary friend idea.

Hit record and I want you just start talking about what you want out of your life and why. If you want to lose weight, for example, then state that and talk about why you want to lose weight. Don't be embarrassed and be honest with yourself. If you want to lose weight because your self-esteem suffers because of your size then say so. If you want to lose weight because of health concerns then talk about that along with the reasons you're concerned. If you just want to look good at the next high school reunion then express that!

The more you talk, you'll begin to visualize what you want and your mood will begin to change. You may even catch yourself smiling as you talk about what changes you want to make. Another point I'd like to make is that this exercise will also bring to the surface whatever has been keeping you from losing weight, starting your own business, taking that dream vacation, saving money, buying a home etc. When that happens you will know what inspires you to change. You will know what drives you to become the person you've always known you could be. If you find yourself getting emotional, make a mental note of that because that is a snapshot of what you want in your life more than anything else!

There's no time limit as to how long you should record or what areas you should cover. Just go with the flow and when you're done play the session back. Listen to it as many times as you need to. Your recorded thoughts will motivate and inspire you to get busy and make your thoughts a reality.

Next it's time to write everything down.

Motivation - Get It In Writing!

The reason that writing out your goals is so essential is because when you take this step it creates a higher level of importance in your mind. We've all been conditioned to get almost everything we do in writing. When you purchase something from a store they give you a written or printed receipt in case you need to return an item. Many professions require their employees to have a written contract before they can work for certain companies. Contractors can't build you a brand new house until they have something in writing detailing what is expected of them.

I could go on and on but you get the idea. The written word carries a lot of weight in our society and so should your goals and plans for your life. In order to keep yourself from getting overwhelmed you're going to use the recording you made earlier as a guide to help you put your goals down on paper. This will help to increase your motivation because you'll be able to look at your list and instantly feel inspired to maintain your momentum and keep moving forward.

How To Write Your Plan/Goals

1. Get pen and paper or use your computer.

2. Create a list of different areas of your life you want to change. So for example you include a list that looks like the following:

Spiritual
Career
Hobbies
Financial
Vacations
Marriage
Children
Health & Fitness

3. Next to each area write what you want to change in those areas or what you want the end result to be when it's all said and done.

Next we'll work on making a detailed to-do list that will move you in the direction of success!

Make YOUR List

Everyone is different. How are you inspired? What things inspire you to get up and get moving towards the things you want on YOUR motivational to-do list?

If you've been following along step-by-step, you should be feeling a lot more motivated and eager to continue on with the process. You have a recording of what you want in your life. From this recording you have written down your goals and now you're going to use what you've written down to list what inspires you.

I call it **Your Motivational To-Do List**

Tools

1. Pen and paper or your computer.
2. Have your written list of goals handy.
3. Get your recording and keep it nearby.

Number your page from one to ten. Then next to each number, beginning with number one, you're going to write what inspires you to get up and take action towards the things you want most in your life and why. These are the things, places and people that are so important to you in your life that you would do whatever it takes to achieve the goals in those areas.

Get the idea?

Here's an example of what your list might look like.

My Motivational To-Do List - The things that inspire me the most in my life.

1. The wonderful sense of relief I get when I maintain a consist relationship with God through meditation and prayer motivates me to focus on my spiritual growth even more. (Next write what you're committed to doing to strengthen your spiritual growth.)

2. The happiness and well-being of my children inspires me to work harder toward starting my own business so that I can provide for their future. (A detailed account of what kind of business you want to start and how you plan to succeed.)

3. I am inspired by others in my field and I take time to educate myself more so I can move up in my company. I'll use the extra income to put toward starting my own business. (Here you should include the course work you need and what the requirements are to get certified if relevant.)

4. Watching and learning about foreign lands inspires and motivates me to plan for a trip of a lifetime around the world! (Get the details you would need regarding costs, airlines, passports, visas and other information to plan for your trip around the world!)

5. The chance to have a healthy body and look great too inspires me to get serious about my weight and get control of my eating. (Then write down the details of what your weight loss plan will be.)

Your list will be a lot more detailed but this should give you a good starting point.

Once you've completed your Motivational To-Do List it's time to put some strategies to work to help you increase your motivation so you can achieve the goals and plans on your list.

Strategies For Getting Motivated

When you have a strategy in place to help increase your motivation you're more likely to maintain your momentum and you'll be more likely to achieve your goals and execute your plans.

In the next sections you'll find several different strategies to choose from. You will probably want to combine several strategies for the maximum effect.

Strategy 1: Staying Spiritually Motivated
Strategy 2: Creating A Special Journal
Strategy 3: Creating A Vision Board
Strategy 4: The Sound Of Music!
Strategy 5: Support Groups
Strategy 6: Motivational Sermons
Strategy 7: Rewards
Strategy 8: Set Smaller Goals First
Strategy 9: Let Others In On Your Goals/Plans
Strategy 10: Save Some Of The Fun For Later
Strategy 11: Keep Track Of Your Goals
Strategy 12: Pick One BIG Goal
Strategy 13: Let Your Imagination Keep You Motivated
Strategy 14: Find Others To Pattern Yourself After
Strategy 15: Make A Commitment To Work On Your Dreams Every Day
Strategy 16: Never Give Up
Strategy 17: Don't Procrastinate
Strategy 18: Monitor Your Thoughts
Strategy 19: Meditation
Strategy 20: Curl Up With A Motivating Book

Okay let's get going!

Strategy 1: Staying Spiritually Motivated

As a Christian, I find that when I focus on the fact that I believe that God has a purpose for my life (and I believe He does for yours too), it is way easier for me to see beyond harder times to a different kind of future.

You may not share my Christian beliefs, but perhaps you are motivated by things of a spiritual nature. I think everyone feels some type of peace when they are connected with the thought that there is something bigger beyond ourselves that we may not be able to see or touch.

Whatever this is for you, connecting with it on a regular basis can greatly center your thoughts, actions and life in general.

My own experience leads me to try to carve out a time each day (typically first thing in the morning) to read my bible and/or do a bible study and spend some time in prayer and worship.

If you are not comfortable with the idea of praying but you do appreciate the idea of quieting your mind, you might want to look at the strategy involving meditation as it can definitely have a similar effect.

Strategy 2: Creating A Special Journal

The biggest advantage to keeping a journal is that it allows you to keep a detailed account of what is going on in your life as you're going about your daily activities. You'll use your journal to record what happens as you're working on your goals. This will help you to stay motivated each day.

How To Use Your Journal

1. When you achieve something on your to-do list that brings you closer to your goal write a "congratulations" to yourself and write down how good it felt to complete the item.

2. If you fail to get something done or stay motivated at times, write it down in your journal. Write why you're feeling down and what happened that day to cause you to lose your motivational spirit.

3. Keep your journal with you at all times.

Now the next time you're feeling down and not inspired to work on your goals, open your journal and find a day where you had a bad day and read what you did to cheer yourself up. Look for any events that have sabotaged your motivation time and time again. For example, you might notice after reading your journal that every time you have a long meeting at work, you become irritable and you avoid working on your goals. Prepare yourself mentally before your next scheduled meeting by reading your list of things that inspire you. Or listen to your recording where you talked about your dreams and goals and let that inspire you.

Your attitude going into the meeting will carry you through the meeting and allow you to avoid having a "motivational break down" later.

Strategy 3: Creating A Vision Board

Vision boards are a great way to keep you motivated on what you want in your life by using images that remind you of your goals and plans. To keep yourself motivated here are a few simple ways to create your vision board.

How To Create A Basic Vision Board

Tools

1. Poster board or cork board from your local drugstore or office supply store

2. Pack of colored markers

3. Scissors

4. Push pins for the cork board/tape for the poster board

5. Photographs of loved ones and friends.

6. Magazines with images that represent what you want in your life. For example, pictures of foreign countries you want to visit, homes, cars etc...

Take your poster board, photographs and images from magazines and place them on your poster board or cork board. You can get as creative as you like. Write your name under the car of your dreams or write the date you plan to travel to Spain as examples. Put the pictures of your children and spouse and other photos that inspire you everyday front and center where you can see them.

Place your vision board where you can see it every day. Seeing your dreams represented visually will help you feel motivated to keep working on your plans every single day.

Creating A Vision Board On Your Computer

Tools

1. A PC, Mac or Tablet

2. Images and photo

Use your computer to create a vision board. You don't need special software. You can create your board using simple image software already installed on your computer. Arrange your images the same as you would using an actual poster board adding motivational messages for yourself and anything else you need to stay motivated.

You might also want to check out the very cool social site called Pinterest for another easy way to create visual boards online of the things that inspire you the most.

Strategy 4: The Sound Of Music!

When you're having a bad day and not feeling very inspired about anything, listening to music that makes you feel good about yourself can be a powerful ingredient that can get you right back on your positive motivational track.

Choosing Music

Since everyone's taste in music is different, only you can determine what kind of music uplifts your spirit. Whatever your choice, try to stick with music that has positive lyrics that focus on dreaming big and positive possibilities in life.

Every genre of music has artists who have produced great sounding uplifting music and there are way too many to list here.

How To Find Positive Music in Any Category

You can search on iTunes, Amazon.com and dozens of other websites for music you can purchase and download to your mp3 player, computer or smartphone. Create your own motivational album with music from different artists in as many different genres as you want. Then once you have the mix of music you're happy with, listen to your music whenever you're feeling uninspired. Make it a point to get back to working on your plan. You can even listen while you work on your game plan to get an extra added motivational boost.

Music Categories

Gospel
Christian Rock
Classical
Pop
Rock
R&B
Adult Contemporary
Latin

Another category that has a lot of inspiring music is from movie soundtracks. Some soundtracks feature beautiful music performed by some of the world's best orchestras.

Strategy 5: Support Groups

Support groups are everywhere these days. You can find groups that meet regularly and as often as every week. Getting together with like-minded individuals to help you stay motivated is a great way to keep yourself from giving up on your dreams and goals.

Where To Find Support Groups

1. Check your church or other places of worship.

2. Community centers and nonprofit organizations in your area

3. The Small Business Administration may have information on local groups to help you stay focused if you're trying to start your own business.

4. Check with your local library as they may have information on groups near you.

5. Local community colleges are also a great place to find support.

Online

Do a search online for support groups that either meet locally or via online chat groups, teleconferences and web conferences.

Start Your Own

If you have the time and interest you could start your own support group. You could also consider creating your own mastermind group. A mastermind group is a group of like-minded individuals all focused on achieving the same goals. Usually mastermind groups focus on starting your own business, achieving goals or maintaining a positive mindset.

Strategy 6: Motivational Sermons

I love listening to sermons that uplift, motivate, make me smile and feed my spirit! Joel Osteen, TD Jakes and several others have some of the most motivating sermons I've ever heard. If you can't watch sermons when they air on television because of your schedule, you can typically access replays to watch for free on their websites and most also have podcasts you can download and listen to any time.

If you find your faith beginning to wane, watching an uplifting sermon from your favorite pastor can be the spiritual shot in the arm you need to get you refocused again.

How To Find Motivational Sermons

1. You can purchase sermons from your favorite pastors directly from their websites or major sites like Amazon.com.

2. Search online via Google or Bing

3. If you have a DVR you can record sermons so you can watch at a time that's more convenient for you.

Free Video Sermons/Inspiring Christian Stories & Movies

1. YouTube

2. Gospeltube.com

3. Lightsource.com

4. Christianforecasters.com

5. Godvine.com

If Christian sermons are not your thing, you can also find plenty of other motivational speeches and talks online using the same types of resources.

Strategy 7: Rewards

Rewarding yourself as you move along with your plans is another way to keep yourself motivated. This works especially well if your goals will take an extended amount of time to come to fruition. Create a reward system to congratulate yourself when you're successful and even when you're not so successful in completing a goal. The point is to give yourself a pat on the back for reaching a goal while also keeping you motivated when you miss the mark from time to time. You're not rewarding failure, you're rewarding yourself for sticking to your plan and giving it your all.

Rewards

You can decide the kinds of rewards you wish to treat yourself with, but here are a few ideas.

1. A spa day

2. Dinner at your favorite restaurant

3. Treat yourself to a new outfit

4. A day trip to tour wineries, orchards or something similar

5. A book from your favorite author

6. Cologne or perfume

7. Invite friends over for a BBQ

8. Get a make over

9. Learn a new skill

10. Go to a movie or play

I'm sure you can think of a lot of different things you can do to reward yourself. Just make sure you do so consistently. Even though you're the one giving yourself a reward, the anticipation of getting a reward will help you to stay motivated. If you tell yourself you're going to reward yourself with a trip to a day spa if you successfully stick to your plan everyday for a a week, you're going to be feeling more motivated to actually achieve that goal.

Strategy 8: Set Smaller Goals First

Sometimes having too many goals can be so overwhelming that trying to keep up with them all can cause one to feel like giving up. By setting smaller goals first, you can stay motivated without feeling like you have to do everything at one time in order to be successful.

How To Set Smaller Goals

Bigger goals can take longer to reach and during that time you may get discouraged because it's taking too long. By setting smaller goals that lead to your ultimate goal you will be more inclined to achieve successes along the way which can help you to stay motivated.

1. Pick a major goal you're trying to reach.

2. Decide on smaller goals that you have to reach to get to that bigger goal. For example, if you're afraid of heights and your goal is to get over your fear by going skydiving for the first time in your life, you could first take a few jumps in a simulated skydiving facility instead. This will make you feel inspired to stay focused on your ultimate goal no matter how long you have to wait until you make the actual big jump

Do these steps with each of your goals and you won't get distracted while you're working toward your bigger goals.

Strategy 9: Let Others In On Your Goals/Plans

If you really want to stay motivated in a big way gather up all your friends and family and let them know what your biggest goal is and how you plan to achieve it. Then schedule time at a future date to show them how much you've actually achieved.

If you choose this strategy, you will be highly motivated to do what you told your family and friends you would do. It does create more pressure on you to execute your plans, but it also keeps you extremely motivated. The last thing you want to do is face your family and friends and tell them you gave up!

How To Share Your Goals With Others

1. Have an informal gathering of your closest friends and family.

2. Make it festive and fun.

3. Pick an appropriate moment to announce to everyone what your plans, dreams and goals are and when you plan to achieve them.

It will be up to you to stay on track and stay focused so you can report your successes later. This kind of accountability can be a great motivation for some people.

Strategy 10: Save Some Of The Fun For Later

When you're working on your goals, try not to schedule the things that are the most fun all at once. Spread some of the fun throughout the process. The fun can be the different steps and/or rewards that you give yourself during your goal process.

The best way to stretch out your fun is to set up a reward schedule first, (see Strategy 7: Rewards) then take a look at your schedule and see where you can work in rewards.

When you run into periods where you're not checking off your goals as fast as you would like, you'll need to take a break and take advantage of one of your fun rewards to make you feel better and prepare yourself to get back to your plan and keep moving forward.

Strategy 11: Keep Track Of Your Goals

Keeping track of your goals will give you the opportunity to measure just how well you're doing as you go along. Invest in a simple notebook or special calendar and write down each milestone. On days when you're not doing so well with your goals you can look at your previous accomplishments and feel inspired again knowing you have the ability to achieve your goals because you've done so many times before. That will give you a lot of motivation and encouragement to keep going.

Strategy 12: Pick One BIG Goal

Choosing one major goal instead of trying to complete several at once can be the biggest factor in giving you the positive motivation to excel in other areas of your life as well.

The Top 3 Tips To Choosing One Big Goal

1. Take a look at every area of your life and determine out of all of your goals which one you consider to be the biggest goal of them all. For me it was losing 100lbs!

2. Once you decide on your biggest goal, use the tips in the Motivation - Getting A Clear Picture and in the Motivation-Get It In Writing sections to come up with the plan to get what you want.

3. Stay the course until you've achieved the desired result. The motivation and drive you'll have once you reach the finish line will make you even more motivated to take on more goals.

You will be unstoppable!

Strategy 13: Let Your Imagination Keep You Motivated

When you feel like you're not getting any closer to your goals and your motivation starts to decrease, it's time to harness the power of your imagination!

How To Use Your Imagination To Keep You Motivated

1. When things aren't going as planned find a quiet place where you can relax undisturbed.

2. Imagine yourself achieving your goals and celebrating!

3. Think about how much better your life and the life of others will be because you didn't give up.

4. Then recommit yourself to focusing on your goals.

You'll find that this technique is great for putting you back into a positive mood and not allowing yourself to get bogged down in your own "pity party". Instead you'll feel empowered and your motivation to succeed will return.

Strategy 14: Find Others To Pattern Yourself After

When you need a boost to your motivation, find others who have already achieved what you want to achieve. If you know someone personally spend some time asking them questions about how they were able to succeed. Ask them how they dealt with failure and what it was that made them not give up. Use their inspiring stories to fuel your own journey and that will help you to increase your motivation.

Search The Internet

If you don't know anyone on a personal level, search online for stories you can read about. Print them out and post them where you can see them every day. The next time you want to quit, reach for one of those inspiring stories, read it out loud and say to yourself, "If they did it, so can I!"

Documentaries

You can also look for documentaries about people who, despite great odds, achieved big dreams. Watch and see what you can learn from others and use whatever methods strike a chord within you.

Strategy 15: Make A Commitment To Work On Your Dreams Every Day

Working on your dreams can be the ultimate motivator. If you make a point to do even something small every day that will bring you closer to getting what you want in your life, soon enough it will become a habit that you look forward to. You'll enjoy seeing your new life unfold one day at a time.

Choose One Small Goal Each Day

1. It doesn't matter what you do because every step is connected to your ultimate goal.

2. Celebrate your commitment!

3. Look forward to the results.

Strategy 16: Never Give Up

Not one person who is successful got that way because he or she quit!

Remember that when you think you're ready to throw in the towel. While it's true that there will be a few bumps in the road, there are steps you can take to deal with problems before they happen.

How To Stay Motivated When You're Ready To Quit!

Like it or not, "stuff" will happen. If you prepare yourself ahead of time for those times when everything seems to go haywire, you'll come out ahead in the end.

1. Prepare yourself mentally and emotionally for setbacks and disappointments.

2. To help you deal with letdowns, always have something inspiring to read, listen to or watch.

3. This will get you back to a mental and emotional place of safety so you don't let negativity take over.

Strategy 17: Don't Procrastinate

Procrastination is a dream assassin! If you want to completely do away with your goals and plans, procrastination is a quick and efficient way of doing just that.

How To Avoid Procrastination And Stay Motivated

1. When you're working on your dreams and you find yourself putting things off that you know you should complete, you've got to ask yourself a simple question..."is my decision to put this off until later going to bring me closer to my goal or further away?'

2. Then get up and take action! Choosing to take action right then and there is the absolute best way to stop the habit of procrastination from destroying your dreams.

3. Once you refuse to take the easy way out by not doing what you know you should, your level of motivation will go through the roof!

Strategy 18: Monitor Your Thoughts

Keeping your thoughts focused on positive scenarios as much as possible is imperative to keeping your motivation up. If you find your thoughts wandering and you begin to question whether or not you can really reach your goals, take the following steps to re-set your mind and get re-motivated.

How To Keep Your Thoughts Focused On The Positives

1. If you find yourself engaging in negative self talk about your ability to achieve your goals, mentally say the word STOP in your mind. Then replace your negative self talk with something positive instead. (If you are a Christian, you might opt to recite a favorite bible verse that you find comforting to quiet your mind.)

2. When you begin to doubt yourself and the choices you're making, immediately disrupt that train of thought by telling yourself you're not going to sabotage what you've been working hard to accomplish. Remind yourself how smart and confident you are and smile until you begin to feel better.

3. When your motivation is weak, if you are a Christian turn to God and pray for strength to get you through the turmoil and give thanks for the miracles you are about to experience! If you don't practice a particular faith, but you are spiritual, turn to meditation or whatever practices help you to connect to your spiritual self.

Strategy 19: Meditation

Meditation has been around in various forms for thousands of years. Regular practitioners report leading happier, calmer lives because of their meditation practice. By calming your spirit, you automatically calm your mind and staying motivated is no longer a struggle.

You can find some guided meditations to follow online or for purchase. There are also books and programs that can offer information as to how to develop this type of practice in your life.

Your local gym or spiritual center might also offer some type of group meditation. Along with meditation you might want to think about looking into the various types of yoga practices.

As a Christian I meditate on the word of God to keep me motivated and if you can relate to this, your bible along with some worship music might provide everything you need to enjoy the powerful effects of meditation.

Strategy 20: Curl Up With A Motivating Book

Reading a book that inspires you to take action and motivates you to dream bigger and go for what you want 110%, can have lasting long term effects on your motivational levels.

Reading For Motivation

1. If you are a Christian, you know that the Bible is a rich resource of motivation to last a lifetime!

2. There are several books filled with motivational quotations from hundreds of philosophers, religious figures, politicians and people from all walks of life. Search on Amazon to find motivational books to inspire you.

3. Find verses from the Bible and quotation books and post them where you can see them each day.

4. You could also choose to read a new motivational quote each morning when you wake up to set the tone for the rest of your day.

5. Whenever you're feeling uninspired reach for a quote or something uplifting to read to turn your mood around.

Note that if you are not into reading, there are many motivational books available on CD or as downloadable MP3 so this might be another option for you to consider.

Increased Motivation WILL Lead To Big Change

Sending you out with one last little cheering session...Keep after it and motivation will lead to action which will lead to huge momentum in your life!

I hope you're feeling a lot more confident by now and you're ready to get started on your goals and getting more out of your life than ever before. You now have several strategies you can use to increase your motivation, but you have to put them to practice. You've got to make staying positively motivated a lifestyle.

If you stay committed to the importance of being positively motivated, you will automatically take action. That action will open the floodgates of momentum that will propel you into a happier more joyful life!

I leave you with this great quote:

"We are what we repeatedly do; excellence then is not an act but a habit."
~ Aristotle

How to Be Healthier: A Blueprint for Creating a Healthy Lifestyle

Feeling Good Physically Is THE Most Important Thing

Without Your Health You Have Nothing!

There's a lot to be said about the importance of leading a healthy life. I know it can get confusing and overwhelming. It seems like every time you turn on the television there's yet another report about the dangers of eating this food and that food and how obesity is becoming an epidemic in our society. As the title above states so simply, without your health you have nothing. All the wealth in the world means nothing if you can't enjoy the simple pleasures of life because of poor health.

Making Good Health Your #1 Priority

Every year we all make a long list of resolutions and one of the most common is to get in shape and lead a healthier lifestyle. The problem is, most of us do a lot of talking and if we're lucky we keep that resolution for maybe a couple of weeks and then it's back to our old habits of poor eating. The only exercise we get is the 30 second walk from our front door to the car. The consequences of not taking better care of our health are clear.

Too much saturated fat, sugar and refined carbohydrates in our diet (also smoking, drugs, alcohol and stress) can lead to:

- Increased likelihood of heart disease
- High blood pressure
- Stroke
- Certain cancers
- Diabetes
- High cholesterol
- Severe depression
- Obesity
- Alcoholism
- Drug abuse

Unless you have a history of certain health problems in your family, you have the ability to avoid many of the maladies mentioned above by making the decision to change the way you think about your health. I don't want you to feel like I'm picking on you, but this is about you and your health and I want to be sure you're really paying attention. If you're not as fit and healthy as you know you could be right now but you feel pretty good so you don't think too much about it, you're playing a bit of a game of Russian Roulette with your health.

One of the reasons people feel blindsided when their doctor tells them that their blood pressure is so high that they could have a stroke at any time, or that their weight gain is making their heart work too hard, is because it never occurred to them to make leading a healthier life a priority goal in their lives. When you are more aware of and actively involved in staying fit, you pay closer attention to what your body is trying to tell you. If you're not aware, you are more than likely to simply ignore the signs of ill health.

Make Living Healthier Your Main Goal BEFORE You Have No Other Choice

It's common that many people who start working out and changing their diet after being a couch potato for so long, have changed their ways because they've had some kind of health scare. If you've read my book on " How To Be Motivated: A Blueprint for Increasing Your Motivation" you're already familiar with the scenarios that motivate us to do what we do each day of our lives. Being told to change your diet or risk losing your life is a very powerful motivator!

Now, just imagine if you stopped waiting until something bad happened to make good health a priority. What if you decided that right now you're going to break the mold and start setting health goals for yourself?

How much could your life change now and in the future from that one decision? I can tell you from experience, the differences will be life changing! I can speak to this personally because after I made the decision to lose 100+ lbs my life changed in ways I could have never, ever imagined. I thank God every day for leading me to take action and responsibility for my own health. It's not always easy - and I am still on that journey today - but through faith, prayer and a lot of hard work I've made a lot of progress. In my other series "How To Lose 100 Pounds", I give you a step-by-step blueprint for setting goals and tips related to weight loss. If you have a lot of weight to lose, you may want to check that out. (More info on that at the end of this book.)

Are You Ready To Make Good Health A Priority In Your Life?

I wrote this blueprint about creating a healthier life because I've benefited from making the same choice I'm asking you to make right now. I would love nothing more than to get an email from you telling me how much better your life is because you made the decision to set goals for your health. If you're willing to commit to giving it your all, I promise you will never look at life the same way again.

When you feel good physically and you live a healthier life everything else seems to fall into place. All you need is a plan and a set of goals to work towards. Grab a pen and paper or your computer and get ready to write your own personal blueprint for creating a healthy lifestyle!

How To Choose Your Health Goals

What is the biggest challenge you're facing in terms of your health and fitness right now?

This is a question you should spend a little time thinking about before you answer it. Sometimes the answer isn't as easy as you might think. One way to decide is to make a list of any health issues you have. Just jot down whatever comes to mind. If you're married or have someone close to you, ask them to help you, especially when it comes to deciding if weight is a problem. You may think you're only carrying "a few extra pounds" but the reality may be a lot different. Others can see things in you that you either don't see or are in denial about and so it's important to have a little extra help.

Once your list is complete, take each item and next to it write the kinds of problems you believe that particular issue is causing in your life. Then write what changes you would like to make and this information will be the goal for that specific health issue. Be as specific and as detailed as you can and feel free to include any feelings you're experiencing as you write this down.

Here's a sample of how to write your list:

1. I've got to lose some weight - I've gained more than 50 lbs in a year. The extra weight makes it harder for me to catch my breath, I can't walk around as much as I used to and most of my clothes don't fit. I would like to lose the 50 lbs, and maybe even more. Let's say a total of 75 lbs would be ideal for me.

2. I eat too much fatty foods - I know my diet is why I've gained so much weight and my doctor told me my cholesterol is way too high. I need to change the foods I'm eating to lose weight and bring my cholesterol down to a normal range.

3. Smoking a pack of cigarettes a day! - The smoking is bad for my health, I'm always coughing and my husband is constantly telling me I smell like tobacco. I would like to stop smoking or at the very least reduce it from a pack a day to maybe one half pack a day? I don't know if I can do that just yet.

Focus On The Biggest Goal First

Trying to decide which goal is the biggest when it comes to your health can be difficult, but an easy way to figure it out is to take each issue and all of the things you've written down and read each one out loud slowly. As you're reading them, pay attention to how you're reacting to each one. No matter how hard we try, if we're not being truthful about something to ourselves or others, our bodies will respond accordingly. This can be true if we're having a hard time accepting something we've been told about ourselves.

This is how the FBI trains their agents to spot when a suspect is lying about something. Ask any professional poker player how they know when someone is holding a Royal Flush or not and he or she will explain all about what they call "tells." Tells, are physical reactions we all have to various things. Often we're not even aware of our own "tells". For example, every mother knows when their child isn't being honest about something because of the tone of their voice or the way they bite their fingernails every time they're being less than truthful. These habits follow us into adulthood.

So as you're reading, your body may literally tell you which goal to focus on first.

If, for example, you're reading about eating too much fatty foods and your body language barely changes that's probably not your biggest goal. If, on the other hand, as you're reading something about losing weight and you begin to shift your body weight or you begin too feel uncomfortable, you're probably looking at your first goal to work on.

Another way to help yourself figure out which goal you should focus on first is by again reading each issue out loud to yourself, then for each one ask yourself this question.

"What could happen if I don't take the time to change this?"

Then say out loud what the consequences could be... if, for example, you don't stop smoking and continue with a pack a day. Think about how your choices not only affect you, but also how they may impact those you love.

Check With Your Doctor First

It's always a good idea to make an appointment with your physician first before making major changes in your diet and exercise routine. Once you've completed the exercise for choosing your biggest health goal, share it with your doctor and let him or her know what you want to change. Your doctor may decide to do a complete blood workup to document your cholesterol levels and check for any abnormalities that could be worsened if you make any major lifestyle changes to your diet. He or she will also check your blood pressure to make sure it's okay to eat certain foods or eliminate others.

If you have some concerns about your health, your doctor visit might also include a complete stress test to make sure your heart is strong enough for physical activity. They can also be checking for any physical limitations that may prevent you from performing certain exercises. If you've had a previous injury or surgeries you're doctor is unaware of be sure to mention this as well.

Finally, never add any kind of supplements to your diet without checking with your doctor first, especially if you are taking any kind of prescription medications. If you do decide to take supplements, ask a pharmacist if there are any known negative side effects when taken with whatever medications you may be on currently.

Basic Areas Of Optimal Health

Putting It All Together

Leading a healthy lifestyle and making the decision to make it a priority is absolutely fantastic and I am so proud of you for making that choice. Just like any other goal in your life, you will be more likely to succeed if you prepare yourself well before you begin the actual process of changing your lifestyle.

In the next sections, I'll share some basic strategies you can use to get yourself pointed in the right direction. The following areas all contribute to the betterment of your overall health no matter if you're trying to lower your blood pressure, maintain a healthy cholesterol level or lose weight.

Here are the areas that will be covered:

- The importance of eating a healthy diet for weight loss and better health.

- A quick guide to the foods and other things you might want to consider limiting or avoiding altogether.

- Why even basic exercise routines can have an amazing effect on your overall health.

- How getting the proper amount of sleep can make a major difference in your results.

- Water! Why it is such a powerful ally when it comes to staying healthy.

- How managing your stress levels can lead to optimum health and less fat!

- How to develop a personal reward system to help keep you motivated

Get ready to take lots of notes…you've got a healthier lifestyle to create!

Your Diet

Healthy Diet + Consistency = Fantastic Results!

Maintaining a healthy diet is one of the most important things you can do when you're trying to create a healthier lifestyle. The benefits of eating certain foods happens over time, so eating a certain way has to become your new way of eating for the rest of your life. Okay, I know what you're thinking. You assume that eating healthier automatically means the end of great tasting foods. That is so not true! When you learn about the benefits of eating certain foods and learn about healthier ways of making those foods taste good, your taste buds will never be the same!

The key to getting the most benefits from better eating habits, is staying consistent and being patient with yourself. Also be open to trying new foods that you may not be familiar with or eating old favorites in totally new ways.

Creating Your New Diet

Your diet plan is going to be unique to you and also has a lot to do with how much weight you have to lose or changes you need to make to get yourself in better general health. I focus a lot on weight loss because many health issues can be traced back to being overweight. In cases where this is true, once the weight comes off, many of the other issues related to joint pain, blood pressure and even heart issues either decrease significantly or totally disappear. Plus, what you eat the most has a measurable effect on your body's health.

Healthy Foods

Take a look in your cupboard, your freezer and your secret hiding places for diet killing foods. Basically, if you have more boxes of cookies, chips and the like than you do fruits and veggies, it's time to bring in the fat fighting, feel good foods instead!

Here are some handy diet tips you can use to help you reach your health and fitness goals.

117

Fruits & Vegetables

Everything your mother told you about vegetables is true. The amount of antioxidants found in leafy green veggies is a powerful but easy way to help your body prevent certain cancers and keep your body fat percentage low. Adding 5 or more servings of fruits and vegetables a day will provide the right amount of fiber to your diet and improve your health overall. Instead of eating fruits and vegetables as side dishes, make them the star of your meals. Experiment with different spices and flavor combinations or invest in a healthy eating cookbook.

Lean Meats

Make sure you're getting plenty of protein in your diet. Protein feeds your muscles and helps them recover after workouts. You can get protein from many different foods including, fish, chicken breasts, lean beef, beans and nuts.

Things You May Want to Limit

Not Everything That Tastes Good …Is Good For You!

Just as there are plenty of foods you should eat to lose and maintain weight and keep your body in tip-top shape, there are other foods, additives and beverages you should limit or avoid as much as possible.

Let's take a look at a few and the negative side effects of each.

Refined white sugar, white flour, white rice and white bread should all be avoided as much as possible. The reason has to do with the high level of insulin your body has to produce every time you eat one of these refined foods. That's a problem because insulin makes your body store fat. But it doesn't end there. This increased amount of insulin can also lead to heart disease because your triglyceride levels increase. If you're eating these foods in excess, in time your pancreas can simply stop functioning because it can no longer keep up with the demand your body needs because of the high insulin levels. If you are prone to diabetes this is a scenario that could be disastrous for your health.

Bleached flour can cause internal infections and did you know that foods with the word "bleached" in it are actually bleached with chemicals similar to the same bleach you use to keep your clothes looking nice and white? Bread and rice for example are not naturally white…they are brown. Manufacturers bleach these foods because some retailers several years ago thought people wouldn't buy or eat bread or rice if they were brown. You are eating foods with bleach residue and that can't be good for your body at all.

Salt

You need a certain amount salt in your basic diet to help your body function properly. Too much salt can lead to high blood pressure, heart disease and stroke. Among other things it causes you to retain an excess amount of water in your body.

One way to avoid getting too much salt in your diet is to avoid processed pre-packaged foods. They are loaded with high levels of sodium. Fast foods are also high in sodium and fats and should be avoided. There are times you may eat something and be shocked at how much sodium it contains because you didn't taste much salt. Over time we can develop a higher tolerance level to salt and so it's possible you won't even realize just how much salt you're actually eating.

Drugs

Alcohol is considered a drug and if consumed in excess you risk becoming addicted. It is also a depressant and should not be consumed if you are taking prescription medication for depression. This can lead to deadly health issues, such as heart and liver disease and brain damage. An extreme example of what can happen as a result of addiction to alcohol might be divorce, job loss and even jail as some people commit crimes while intoxicated, such as driving drunk. In terms of weight loss, alcohol can derail any weight loss plan and you could end up gaining not only the weight you lost, but additional pounds as well.

Caffeine

Caffeine is another substance that is considered by many to be a drug because it is highly addictive. The more common way to describe caffeine is as a "stimulant" and it is found in hundreds of different foods and drinks. Coffee, tea, chocolate, over the counter supplements to prevent sleep, cold medicines, pain relievers, weight loss supplements and diet pills are some examples of things that contain caffeine. Some side effects associated with caffeine include an elevated heart rate or an irregular heart rate, sweating, increased urination and interference with your ability to sleep. If you are super sensitive to caffeine you may also experience being very "jittery" until the effect wears off. Then you might experience what is known as a crashing sensation that can be very unpleasant and energy depleting.

Although caffeine has been known to aid in weight loss, it only works when used in conjunction with other potentially harmful foreign substances and really it's not worth the side effects and other potential health problem.

Listen, I will be the first to admit that I do not adhere to all of these things 100% or even 70%, to be honest. If you've read any of my books in the "How to Lose 100 Pounds" series you know that I am not real big on the word "diet" or the idea of completely eliminating certain foods in order to lose weight. As someone who has been dealing with a lot of weight to lose, I know that this is a process and sometimes the whole "can't have" food list can totally backfire.

I'm telling you this basic knowledge of what I know to be the "most" healthy so that you can research further and decide the things that you want to implement for yourself.

I am NOT perfect…far from it! I don't expect you to be either.

Exercise

Whether or not you choose to exercise to help with weight loss or not, there's no doubt that exercise is one of the best gifts you can give your body over a lifetime. Combine a regular exercise program with a healthy diet and you've got a recipe for better health, a fitter body and even better emotional and mental health.

It doesn't matter how old you are or how much you weigh, if you engage in regular exercise you will benefit tremendously. Even if you've never exercised a day in your life, you can get into better shape no matter when you start.

The Benefits of Exercise On Your Body

The Heart

Although you can begin exercising at any time in your life, the sooner you start the better, especially when it comes to your heart. Exercise helps your heart perform better, and that can mean normal blood pressure and lower cholesterol levels. Heart attacks can and do happen to those who are considered young as well as to older individuals. Schedule a stress test with your doctor before you start working out, especially if you've never worked out before…just as a precaution.

The Lungs

Your lungs not only allow you to breathe, but they are also responsible for providing oxygen to your blood and the rest of your body. Exercising gives your lungs the ability to perform at their highest level and may actually add years to your life.

Weight Loss & Weight Management

Exercise when done regularly can not only help you lose weight, but it can also help you maintain your weight loss. In addition to keeping those extra pounds off exercise can help you to decrease your chances of diabetes, high blood pressure and certain cancers that tend to be associated with excessive weight.

The Benefits of Exercise When You're Trying To Lose Weight

Stretching

Performing regular stretching exercises both before and after your workout is a very important part of one's routine. This is especially important for warming up your muscles before you engage them in strenuous workouts or when lifting heavy weights. Stretching also prevents injuries because when you lift weights you are stretching your muscles further than you normally would. You can cause injury if your muscle has not been properly stretched prior to lifting weights. The fibers of your muscle can tear too much, resulting in painful muscle strains and sprains.

Weight Training

The biggest benefit to lifting weights is building muscle mass. More muscle throughout your body also helps burn more fat because it helps to increase your metabolism. Increased metabolism results in making your body burn more fat for longer periods of time, even when you're not lifting weights. Other benefits include better self confidence, increased strength and strong bones and joints.

Cardio

In order to lose just one pound of fat you need to burn off 3,500 calories. When you perform some kind of cardio activity like running, walking, bike riding and high intensity training with weights, you are warming up your body which then leads to the burning of calories. Every 30 minutes of continual cardio activity can burn between 150 - 300 calories or more depending on the intensity level of the exercise you are performing. Regular cardio exercise along with diet can help you to lose weight and keep it off for good!

Getting Adequate Sleep

If you're not getting enough sleep, it will not only have an adverse effect on your weight loss but also on your overall health.

The Benefits of Sleep

Your body does a lot 24 hours a day. Your organs, such as your heart, kidneys and liver are constantly working to keep you healthy and alive. There are specific cells in your body which act like your body's personal police department by attacking intruders in the form of viruses to get rid them before they can do harm to you. Your brain is like a conductor, constantly communicating to your entire central nervous system making sure everything is working as it should. This includes the functions of digesting your food and preparing it for elimination. Your brain also lets you know when you're hungry or sends you a sign that you body needs some kind of medical attention when things go wrong.

So it's no wonder that your body requires a lot of rest in the form of sleep. If you're not getting enough sleep you may feel irritable, have headaches, loss of appetite and difficulty concentrating on even simple tasks. If you're working out regularly you body will require rest to repair your muscles and regain strength afterwards so that you'll be able to work out at a higher level at your next exercise session.

The Consequences of Not Getting Enough Sleep

In the long term a lack of regular sleep can contribute to obesity, blood pressure problems, increased risk of breast cancer, heart disease, colon cancer and diabetes. Extended periods where you are not sleeping can also cause mental and emotional problems.

Most experts agree that the average adult should get between 8 and 10 hours of sleep a night.

How To Make Sure You're Getting Enough Sleep

If you're not sleeping well, be sure to check with your doctor and schedule a check-up to make sure your lack of sleep is not being caused by an unknown serious medical condition. If your doctor gives you a clean bill of health, you probably need to change your routine.

1. Make sure you refrain from doing anything too stimulating before bedtime that might interfere with your ability to sleep. Examples of this might include watching high action movies or engaging in other activities that get you ramped up to the point that you are too excited to sleep.

2. Try going to sleep and getting up at the same time every day including on your days off.

3. Avoid eating or drinking anything with caffeine or anything else that is considered a stimulant.

4. Sleep in a dark environment with little to no light. Light causes your brain to signal your body to wake up when too much light is present. Too much light can also interfere with your ability to sleep soundly.

5. Try to avoid taking sleep medications unless prescribed by a doctor. There are over the counter products that will put you too sleep but most will also make you feel "over tired" because the effect of the drug itself hasn't completely worn off when it is time for you to wake up. Over the counter sleep meds are not known to be addictive, however prescription sleep medications are known to be highly addictive.

Drinking Water

Water...You Can't Live A Healthy Life Without It!

The human body is primarily made of water. Every person has a different percentage of water in their body but generally about 60% of your body is made up of water. Your brain is about 70% water. When you think of it in those terms it's easy to see why drinking a lot of water each day it vital to your overall health and your ability to lose weight. You are constantly losing water through sweating, elimination and just by breathing.

How Much Water Should You Drink?

Drinking 6 - 8 glasses of water each day is essential to your good health. If you're working out regularly you can add additional water to what would be considered the norm. Your muscles are made up of about 70% water and needs water to form. Fat, on the other hand, is only about 20% water. If you're not drinking enough water your body will begin to go into survival mode and hold on to the water. That's where the term water weight comes from. Our bodies are designed that way to keep us from doing harm unintentionally. Your body thinks it's not going to get enough water to sustain itself because you're not drinking enough so it automatically begins to reserve water. To stop your body from reserving water you simply need to drink more water every day. Eventually, you'll begin to lose your water weight.

The Benefits of Drinking Water

Bodily Functions

Water helps ALL of your organs and other functions to operate at the highest level capable for your body. You need water to move nutrients from one part of your body to the other parts. Water is essential to proper digestion and without enough water you can become constipated. Oxygen is like food for your cells and water helps your cells absorb the oxygen they need. Water helps prevent dehydration which can cause headaches, fatigue and circulation problems with your blood.

Water Helps Your Body Maintain Temperature Controls

When you are in hot weather water helps keep your body from overheating and the opposite is true when you are cold. Water helps to keep your body temperature from dropping too low.

You Look Marvelous Darling!

When you reach your weight loss goals you also want to look good too. Your skin is 90% water and well hydrated skin moisturizes your skin naturally from the inside out.

Reducing Stress

Stress

No matter who you are or what you do for a living, stress plays a role in your life in some way. It's nearly impossible to live in a modern society and not have stress on some level. The big issue with stress is the kind of stress you have and if the amount of stress is so great that it can be detrimental to your health.

What Causes Stress

Family issues, job pressures or job loss, divorce, death of a loved one, financial issues, excessive worrying etc. are all things that greatly induce stress. Stress can also be caused by events that are otherwise happy and joyful like planning a wedding, graduating from college, interviewing for a job or even working on your goals.

Medical problems are one of the biggest causes of stress. Worrying about getting well or the treatment process can be extremely stressful. Those who lead a relatively stress free life can be adversely effected by stress if their health has already been compromised in some way. In this case, stress can actually make their condition even worse. Even medical procedures like surgeries can cause physical stress to the body itself as it works to repair and heal itself.

The Effects of Stress When You're Trying To Lose Weight

Stress can cause you to lose weight but not in a healthy manner. Some people who are under a lot of stress may experience a loss of appetite which then leads to weight loss. Several studies suggest that if you're dealing with a high level of stress in your life it can sabotage your ability to lose weight as well and even cause you to gain more weight in some instances.

Tips To Manage Stress

1. Meditation can be a simple but powerful way to relax and manage stress to keep it from becoming a major problem in your life.

2. Avoid situations whenever possible that you already know cause you to stress out.

3. If you are a Christian, prayer can go a long way in helping you to live a stress free life.

4. Find ways to relax more often. Exercise is a known stress reliever so regular walks can greatly reduce the level of stress that you might feel. Getting regular massages can really help too.

5. Focus your mind on positive things to keep from creating stress in your body which can also be a result of constant negative thinking.

Having Downtime

And The Winner Is…..YOU!

When you're working towards creating and living a healthier lifestyle it takes a lot of planning and commitment on your part. It's like working an extra job and you're the only employee. In order to keep motivated, reward yourself when you reach different milestones.

YOU Decide When & What

You can easily add in ways to make your goal of a healthier lifestyle a lot more fun by setting up when and what your rewards will be ahead of time. This will give you something to look forward to and enjoy during the process.

When you lose a certain amount of weight each month reward yourself with something that makes you feel good about your accomplishment. The reward can be something simple or as expensive as you can afford. This is really up to you.

You can plan to take a vacation to someplace you've always dreamed about once you reach your final goal. Create smaller rewards when you stick to your diet for one week straight and gradually increase the reward the longer you're able to stick to your plan. Have an "I lost 5 lbs This Month Party!" and invite close friends over for a healthy dinner and movies.

Take your time and really think about what makes you laugh and feel good about yourself. Then decide at what points you will reward yourself.

How to Be Confident: A Blueprint for Increasing Your Self-Confidence

Confidence vs Self-Esteem

When it comes to confidence building, I think it's nearly impossible to focus just on confidence without also focusing on self-esteem. It's also pretty common for many to mistake confidence and self-esteem as one in the same. Although each has a different meaning, you can't have one without the other.

Plus, having a lot of confidence doesn't mean your self-esteem is as high as your confidence and vise versa.

Let's take a look at what defines confidence and what defines self-esteem along with examples to give you a better grasp on what makes each different from the other.

What Exactly is Confidence Anyway?

Confidence is all about having a strong belief or giving the perception of believing in your ability to be or do something. It is a certain level of self assurance or trust in the abilities of others to be able to do something as well.

Typical Scenarios

Work
As an example, you can have a lot of confidence in yourself when it comes to taking on a new job. Your employer could have confidence in you and trusts that you have the ability to get a specific task done. When someone trusts you to get a task done without supervision, for example, it is usually because they have confidence in you and aren't concerned about something going wrong.

There are various degrees of confidence as well. The level of confidence you have in yourself or others is usually based on something measurable. Using our example of an employer, if you performed a specific task well in the past your employer has a certain amount of "trust" or "confidence" that if given the same or similar task again, you will be able to complete it without problems.

Religion
Confidence in a particular religion can also be described as having unshakable faith. For instance, I am a Christian and I am 100% confident in my faith and religious beliefs.

Relationships
Let's look at another example of confidence but this time using relationships. A married couple, at least in a "typical" healthy relationship, establishes a certain level of trust or confidence in each other to remain faithful.

In fact, it is expected, right?

Now if one decides to cheat and the other finds out about it or is just suspicious, the level of confidence or trust will be broken. It will be very difficult for either to feel confident about their marriage going forward.

Fears
Here's another way of looking at how confidence can be defined. Many say that the biggest fear most of us have is the fear of public speaking, yet people do it every day and most do so effortlessly. Those that struggle with public speaking usually lack confidence in themselves and spend a lot of time telling themselves they can't do it for whatever reason.

Someone with seemingly a lot of confidence but is faking it typically has problems with self-esteem. Reread the first paragraph above defining confidence.

See where I mention the word "perception"? Confidence can be faked. Some people pretend to be confident about a situation in order to not appear afraid, weak or incompetent. This too can be traced back to low self-esteem.

So, let's take a look at the definition of self-esteem and a true story of what happened when having low self-esteem changed one man's life forever.

Self-esteem

It's easy to confuse self-confidence and self-esteem but they really are two different things. Let's look at the definition of self-esteem.

While confidence is more about your "belief" in yourself or ability to do something either real or pretending for others, self-esteem is how you truly view yourself and your life. It doesn't matter if it's true or not because it is how you honestly believe yourself to be no matter what. Self-esteem can be healthy and positive or it can be negative.

Low Self-Esteem

Having low self-esteem means you place a higher value on things like time and money of others instead of your own. In other words, when you think another person's time is more important than your own you are putting yourself beneath others. Or allowing someone to take advantage of you even though you know it's wrong can be a sign of low self-esteem. Even young children can develop self-esteem problems if when growing up they are constantly told something negative about themselves.

Self-Esteem Problems Can Take On a Life of Their Own

There was a documentary I saw some years ago about a man serving a life sentence for murder without the possibility of parole. He was very young, about 17 when he committed that crime. Some 20 years later he had completely turned his life around by turning his life over to God. He got his GED and a college degree while serving his time.
This man not only gained the respect of other inmates, he also made quite an impression on the prison staff and even the warden. He spent his days talking to at risk teenagers warning them to not end up where he was. He even counseled other inmates and held regular Bible studies. His turn around was so sincere that even the family of the man he had murdered had forgiven him.

He had done so much good in his life that there was a petition started to ask the governor to grant him parole.

The reporter interviewing him for the documentary asked why his life was so full of trouble at such a young age.

His Story

See, when he was child, his mother constantly told him he was going to end up just like his father. He never knew his father, but his mother never missed an opportunity to tell him how worthless he was.

He said his mother would tell him over and over and over again from the time he was 5 or 6 years old, that he was nothing and would never amount to anything just like his father. She constantly told him he was worthless and that no one cared about him, not even her.

He went on to tell the reporter that after hearing that over and over again he began to believe it was true. Prior to the murder, he had been in and out of trouble but all were petty crimes. Then one day he decided to rob a man at gun point. He said even though the man did not resist and gave him all of his money he shot him anyway.

The reporter asked, "Why didn't you just let him go?"

The man answered "Because it didn't matter, I was nothing, I was worthless and no one cared anyway."

That was one of the most clear examples of having such a low self-esteem about oneself I had ever seen. It took him 20 years to change his view of himself and raise his self-esteem.

Now do you understand the difference between confidence and self-esteem?

You can have a lot of confidence just as this man had when he decided to take a life, but his self-esteem - his view of himself was almost nonexistent.

Self Image

One of the most common areas where self-esteem comes into play is self image. This is often especially true if you're struggling with a weight problem. Overweight kids are ridiculed and bullied so much, their self-esteem and how they think of themselves are painfully low.

Adults suffer the same self-esteem issues as well and have a difficult time enjoying life. A lot of overweight individuals with low self-esteem don't even believe they're worthy of a healthy loving relationship or even a great career.

In each case, the belief that they can't be as happy as others because of their weight often stops them from doing something to change their circumstance. They don't believe they have the ability to lose the weight and so they don't even try. I've been there on my own journey to lose over 100lbs. I had to make a conscious decision to change. If you're struggling with weight, I'll share some tips to help you change your mindset and build your self-esteem. Then you'll be ready to take the necessary steps to lose weight.

In my book series, "How to Lose 100 Pounds", I created a detailed plan that you can use to help get you on the path to losing weight and leading a healthier life.

Healthy Self-Esteem

When you have healthy self-esteem or you view yourself in a more realistic positive way, you don't worry about what others think of you. You value who you are and what you bring to the world. Add in healthy and real self-confidence and you will enjoy a more fulfilling happier life.

Now, before I can help you to become more confident, you'll need to take an honest look at yourself and assess where you are right now in terms of your self-esteem.

Grab paper and pen because in the next section I'm going to ask you some questions about yourself to help you see how high or how low your self-esteem is in certain areas of your life.

One more thing…you have to answer honestly if you really want to become more confident.

Deal?

Great! Let's get started.

How's Your Self-Esteem?

There are several ways to figure out where you are in terms of self-esteem. There are self-esteem tests, evaluations by mental health professionals and other methods that go way beyond the scope of this book.

I am not a therapist, so if you believe you have severe self-esteem issues that are interfering with your quality of life on a major level, please seek the advice of a qualified professional immediately.

My approach to dealing with self-esteem issues comes from either my own experiences or the experiences of others close to me. Overcoming issues within myself has allowed me to recognize some of those same issues in others and offer strategies that, if used properly, can in time raise your self-esteem and increase your confidence as well.

Tips for Checking Your Self-Esteem

Take paper and pen and write down the answers to the following questions and remember, you've got to be honest. Also keep in mind, there's nothing scientific going on here. The goal is for you to take a real look at yourself and hopefully to recognize areas where your self-esteem could use a boost.

After you've gone through each question, I'll share with you a simple method you can use to further determine the areas in your life you may want to focus on.

1. Do you feel like you don't look as pretty or as handsome as others and regularly tell yourself so every chance you get?

2. Do you feel uncomfortable in social situations and avoid talking to strangers because you're afraid you may say something stupid?

3. If you're overweight, do you think the whole world thinks less of you?

4. Do you go out of your way to please others even if you would rather not be bothered but you do so anyway?

5. Do you feel a sense of accomplishment in your life or do you downplay almost everything you do?

6. Does the mere idea of having to speak in front of group of people make you feel uncomfortable?

7. Do you want to try new things, check out new places or even start a new career but you don't even try because you are sure you're going to fail?

8. Are you constantly putting yourself down when you're around family and friends?

9. Do you consider yourself a happy person?

10. Do you have a difficult time owning up to mistakes you've made either with others or yourself?

11. Do you feel your income is good enough or do you feel you don't have the ability to make more money?

12. Do you ever say to yourself or others that you wish you were as smart as a specific person?

13. Do your feelings get hurt easily over seemingly small insignificant things?

14. Instead of trusting yourself to make good decisions, do you look to others to tell you what you should do in various situations?

15. In relationships, either dating or married, do you spend most of your time jumping through hoops to try and make someone love you?

Whew! I know that's a lot to take in but, if you really allow yourself to ask the hard questions and then give yourself permission to answer truthfully you will be one step closer to enjoying your life from a more positive and more confident perspective.

Once you've gone through and answered each question, reread each one and think about how you feel as you do. Check your body language too.

Why?

Let me explain it this way.

No matter what words are coming out of our mouths when we are talking to a close friend, a relative, a coworker, ourselves or even a stranger on the street, often our emotions and our bodies tell more of the truth than the words we are speaking. So observing our body's reaction to each question along with how we feel can really be insightful.

This is the technique used by CIA and FBI agents and other branches of law enforcement. Even high level poker players are known to use body language to see if you're bluffing. They call it your "tells".

As you read each question be aware of how your body responds. When you're uncomfortable about something in any given situation your body tends to react the same way each time. For example, do you tap on the table or some other object whenever you're nervous? Or if you have a child, how is it that you almost always know when he or she isn't being completely honest with you?

You know your child's "tells" because they do it almost every time.

So be aware of how you react physically and make a note of that. This is a clue for you to recognize an area of your life where your self-esteem could use improvement.

Listen, don't get down on yourself if your personal self-esteem assessment shows you need a bigger boost than you thought. You know what? You should pat yourself on the back for having the guts to be honest with yourself. I'm proud of you for taking those difficult steps.

Good job!

Strategies for Boosting Self-Esteem

In the next section I'm going to give you some strategies you can use to raise your self-esteem and pave the way for rebuilding your self-confidence.

It's important to keep in mind, however, that these strategies will only work if you apply them consistently in your life.

Each strategy will address different areas and will include examples to help you apply the ideas in your own life.

I've divided up the areas that are most often associated with low self-esteem issues. This way you can choose only the areas you feel you need the most help in if you like.

What's Covered

Strategy 1: Self Image - Conquering Low Self-Esteem About Body Image

Strategy 2: People Pleaser - Learn How Being a Little Selfish Can Raise Your Self-Esteem

Strategy 3: Mental Diet - How to Stop the "I'm Not Good Enough" Recording in Your Head

Strategy 4: Anger & Sensitivity - How to Rise Above Criticism

Strategy 5: Fear - It's Not the Big Bad Wolf!

Strategy 6: Perfection - How to Stop Trying to be Perfect

Strategy 7: Children - Raising Self-Esteem in Your Child

Most self-esteem issues can be traced back to either something that happened to you or something someone said to you. Words, in particular, can be extremely powerful. For some people, it may take hearing something negative about yourself repeatedly over a long period of time to lower your self-esteem. For others, just hearing something one time is enough to do the trick.

Events that happen to us can also trigger poor self-esteem as well. That's because they are usually very emotional. Getting picked on as a kid or berated by your boss can cause deep feelings of self loathing and can wipe out confidence in yourself.

It's important to deal with your low self-esteem first because a lack of self-confidence can often be tied to self-esteem issues. Remember, having good self-esteem goes hand in hand with building your self-confidence in the long run.

Now, let's get to work!

Strategy 1: Self-Image - Conquering Low Self-Esteem About Body Image

The Issue

We live in a society that constantly pushes images of what is defined as beautiful. We see super models wearing clothing in sizes the average woman can't wear. We are bombarded with infomercials selling products guaranteed to "fix" us.

Gee, most of us didn't even realize we needed to "fix" anything until we started seeing creams to get rid of wrinkles, pills to lose weight fast, undergarments to make us look smaller, hair gel to make our hair fabulous in just days, blinding teeth whiteners, and every exercise contraption for just 3 easy payments of 39.99!

It's no wonder that poor self-esteem tied to body image is such a major issue. Unfortunately, feeling embarrassed about how one's body looks is showing up in children as young as 5 years old. I've included a chapter on raising your child with healthy self-esteem. If you have kids please be sure to read that section.

Specific Problems

Weight Problems

Not every person who is overweight has low self-esteem. There are plenty of men and women who have no problem with being overweight and lead happy lives. Then there are those who are embarrassed and are constantly focusing on how much they weigh and eat.

Why are some overweight individuals fine with their size while many others are not? It all goes back to what each believes about themselves. They have a belief in themselves that doesn't allow their size to dictate their happiness.

That doesn't mean they won't go on a diet. Most likely they do know it's a healthier option. Many will eventually lose the weight or at least give it a try.

Is This You?

Are you afraid to wear certain kinds of clothes because you worry about what others will say?

Are you constantly putting yourself down about how much weight you've gained?

Do you avoid social activities because you're embarrassed by the way you look?

If you answered yes to these questions, it's time to work towards change.

The Solution

I can speak from experience when I tell you that I understand where you're coming from. I was obese at 278 lbs when I started my weight loss journey. My self-esteem was shot. But once I made the decision to change, I began to feel SO much better about myself...even after only losing the first 10 lbs! Of course it didn't happen overnight, but that's the thing about change. When you're really ready, you won't focus on the time because you'll be focused on the end result.

1. It may be difficult at first, but to raise your self-esteem you've got to stop looking at size 2 models and comparing yourself to them. Everyone is different but that doesn't mean you're less than anyone else. Accept that fact and instead focus on a diet and exercise program that resonates with you. If you need help on how to get started and what to do, you can find the link to my weight loss series at the end of this book.

2. Exercising will make you feel a lot better about yourself. For one, your body releases "feel good" endorphins when you exercise. Secondly, just thinking about how much healthier you'll be is motivating and makes you feel a lot more positive about yourself.

3. If you're walking around wearing the same clothes you had in the 80's...stop! When you dress in clothes that make you feel good about yourself, your self-esteem gets an almost immediate boost. Get a new look. Maybe a new haircut. Make it a new habit to do something every day that makes you feel better about you.

Here are a few more ideas:

*Surround yourself with people who love and respect you just as you are as a person. Those that encourage and support your decision to make changes can do wonders for your self-esteem.

*Every time you catch yourself comparing your body to someone else, take a moment to change your thoughts to something positive about yourself. Do this every time and soon enough you will stop the habit of always putting yourself down.

*Every day before you get your day started, look at yourself in the mirror and smile. Say out loud, as if you were talking to a friend you care deeply about, something reassuring. For example, "You are a wonderful loving human being and you are beautiful!" I know it might seem a bit corny at first, but give it a try!

Low Self-Esteem and Body Image Can Take Many Forms

Although dealing with excess weight seems to be number one when it comes to self image issues, there are other problems that are related to body image.

The Problem

Poor self-esteem because of the color of your skin, your hair, the size of your nose, your nationality, being considered too short or too tall can all cause issues that lead to confidence problems.

The Solution

*If you're feeling negative about yourself because of your skin color, nationality etc, don't isolate yourself from others like you. Don't run from who you are, instead embrace it. Whoever you are and whatever you believe in, it is a part of who you are as a person.

Realize that you have a rich heritage to share with others. Most of the time people say and do things to others because they don't know anything about you and they may say inappropriate things out of fear. Try introducing yourself and striking up a conversation. Many people will soon realize you're not much different from them and may end up becoming a friend.

You can't change everyone, nor should you try. Just be proud of who you are.

*Talk to others you may know who share similarities with you but who are not worried about how others see them. They may be able to help you see yourself in a more positive light.

If you are the kind of person that is always going overboard to please others, the next strategy to build your self-esteem is for you.

Strategy 2: People Pleaser - Learn How Being a Little Selfish Can Raise Your Self-Esteem

Is This You?

Do you give 150% to your employer, significant other or spouse but get back less than half that effort from others but you never question it?

Do you value the time of others more than you value your own?

Do you end up being the one that always gets in to work before everyone else and stays well after everyone else has gone but rarely are you praised for doing so?

Do you realize you're doing way too much to get others to like you but you don't know how to stop?

You deserve so much better. There's an old saying I heard years ago. "Whatever you chase runs away." I don't remember where I heard that, but it's so simple and so true. Trying to please others and hope that they will like you more is the same as chasing.

So how can you change? Here are a few strategies you can start using right away.

The Issue

People pleasers often suffer from low self-esteem. It's not about just going out of the way to do something for someone. We all take time to help others. In this case, people pleasers jump through hoops and then ask "how high?"

They give up all or most of their time to fix something or wear themselves out trying to make sure others are happy. They may spend money they can't afford in order to buy something for someone, even if the person is only a casual acquaintance. People pleasers will put up with all kinds of people who disrespect them and take advantage of them because they don't want to "rock the boat" or cause any problems.

Why?

People pleasers go over the top because they want others to like them...to be their friend. Some hope that by lowering their own standards and self respect that maybe others will think they're cool and let them be a part of the "clique."

Unfortunately, people pleasers end up getting disrespected and taken advantage of by the very individuals they try so hard to impress. That leaves the people pleaser feeling hurt, used and it can cause a major blow to their self-esteem.

The Solution

1. Get a new set of friends! Not just anybody either. You need to become a lot more selective about who you choose to spend your time with. That may not be possible in a work environment but when it comes to friends, you need find those who appreciate you as a person and don't take advantage of your good nature. You want friends, coworkers and family members who want you around because of who you are and not because of what you can do for them.

2. Learn to just say no. It will feel uncomfortable in the beginning, but if you stay consistent, it will make a world of difference in your life. You need to learn to appreciate the fact that your time is just as valuable as someone else's. There's another saying that says, "We teach others how to treat us."

It may take everyone in your life time to get used to the new you because all they know is the "you" that is always giving up your time to deal with their issues. Hold steady and don't cave. Eventually, they will either get the hint and make adjustments or they will gradually remove themselves from your inner circle.

3. It's easy to get upset when you realize others are enjoying the free ride courtesy of you! The best way to handle that is to control what you will allow from others. That means setting limits on what you will allow from others. You have to speak up and let each one know what is and what isn't acceptable. Not only will you feel your self-esteem turning for the better, you will gain the respect of others and you won't have to jump through hoops any more to get it!

I know it's all a lot to take in, but remember what I said earlier, you've got to be consistent in order to create positive changes.

Low self-esteem issues can be so strong it's like a recording that plays in your head day in and day out.

Does that sound familiar?

In the next section, I'm going to show you how to identify low self-esteem thoughts and give you some ways to get rid of them for good!

Strategy 3: Mental Diet - How to Stop the "I'm Not Good Enough" Recording in Your Head

Is This You?

Do you stop trying to learn new things or maybe even talk yourself out of applying for a promotion at work because you're always thinking that you're not good enough anyway so why waste everyone's time?

Do you often get mad at yourself and frustrated because you messed up on a project or cause problems between you and your spouse or a friend and think about how you can't seem to do anything right?

Do you beat yourself up about something you did even if it was something small and petty?

If you can relate to any of the above your self-esteem has hit an all time low and it's time to do something about it. You can learn how to stop the thoughts you have about yourself and your abilities that say you're not good enough because you ARE good enough!

The Issue

I want you to reread the story in the "Self Confidence vs Self-Esteem" section about the man sentenced to life without parole. It is a clear example of how someone else's opinion, no matter how distorted, can have a devastating effect on a life.

When your self worth is challenged and constantly attacked over and over again, your self-esteem can be damaged so severely that you end up feeling like you no longer matter.

Thoughts & Words

Thoughts, like words, are extremely powerful. This is a great thing when those words and thoughts are positive, but when they are negative they plant themselves in your subconscious and sooner or later you'll begin to have a very self limiting belief about yourself. Your self-esteem withers little by little because of something someone said about you or because of something you tried but failed.

Instead of brushing a comment off or going after whatever it is you want, you absorb all the stuff that brings you down. The next time you try something and fail you start telling yourself you're not good enough and will never be good enough. Soon you start applying this same kind of thinking to everything in your life.

The Solution

1. The next time one of those negative thoughts starts running through your mind, I want you to stop whatever you're doing and replace that thought with something positive. I know it sounds a bit corny, but trust me, if you do so every time not only will those negative thoughts begin to disappear but you will notice your self-esteem growing as well. As a Christian, I find reciting uplifting Bible verses to myself, helps whenever I catch myself doubting my ability to do something. You could do the same thing by writing out affirmations that you could recite to yourself throughout the day.

2. Stop beating yourself up every time you make a mistake. Try to find something that you did right and correct the thing that you had a problem with if possible. Then let it go. If you find yourself falling back into self limiting thoughts immediately find something else to distract your thoughts. Then focus on something positive.

3. Don't let someone else's false opinion of you determine what you believe about yourself. You developed your low self-esteem most likely because someone who was or is very influential in your life either said or did something that stuck with you in a negative way. You don't have to spend your life trying to live up to the standards of others.

Do you get easily offended or hurt when you get even a little bit of criticism from others? Being overly sensitive can be a sign of low self-esteem. There are ways to deal with oversensitivity and anger effectively and that's what we'll deal with in the next section.

Strategy 4: Anger & Sensitivity - How to Rise Above Criticism

Is This You?

Do you get upset when someone tells you to stop being so sensitive?

Do you get so worked up about something someone says about you that you go into full defense mode at the drop of a hat?

Do you find it difficult to accept criticism from others even if it is constructive criticism meant to help you?

The Issue

I chose to lump these two together because in my experience, whenever I've encountered someone who was overly sensitive, it was like walking around on egg shells. One wrong comment and they would get so mad at me or if they made a simple mistake they would walk around being angry with themselves.

This is a very common form of low self-esteem that also takes away your confidence in yourself and others. If left unchecked, it can be the cause of broken relationships with family and friends, job loss and an overall feeling of low self-worth.

Like many self-esteem issues, the reasons you may be overly sensitive could be the result of almost anything in your life. It can begin in childhood or may not develop until adulthood. What's important to focus on now is working on yourself daily to address your issues. Once you acknowledge your anger and sensitivity issues you can begin the process of rebuilding a healthy self-esteem.

The Solution

1. Ask yourself, "Why am I so sensitive about almost everything?" Think about various times throughout your life where you got angry when something was said to you or about you. Think about what was said. Was it something minor?

Then write down what you remember. Try to be as detailed as possible. Once you do that, take a look at what you've written. Look for common things in each situation. For example, was the same person or persons a part of the conversation? Where you talking about the same topic or something related?

By narrowing down some commonalities, you'll begin to see what triggers your anger and why you tend to be so sensitive about some things and not others. This will allow you to recognize similar situations in the future and prepare yourself to control your reactions.

2. The next time someone says something that bothers you, don't overreact especially if you don't agree with what's being said. Instead remain calm and express your opinion. If you feel yourself getting angry, walk away and allow yourself to calm down. If what was being said was truthful, embrace it and do your best to focus on correcting your behavior or actions. It takes time so don't beat yourself up if you don't get this method right away. With practice, you'll get there.

3. The more you deal with your sensitivity and anger issues the stronger your self-esteem will become. Another thing to do is to get into the habit of not letting incidents replay in your mind like a re-run. If you make a mistake and fall back into your old habits, know that it happens, you're only human. Let it go and move on.

It's going to take discipline on your part to check yourself when your sensitivity and anger gets the best of you. Just realize, it's going to take time. If you're committed to change...you can change for the better and you will get there.

Strategy 5: Fear - It's Not the Big Bad Wolf!

Is This You?

Do you avoid speaking in front of crowds or even small groups of people because you're afraid?

Do you wait for others to tell you how to do something even though you already know how but you're afraid you may not be able to get it done the right way?

Are the words "I can't" a part of your everyday belief about yourself in almost everything you do?

The Issue

Fear itself is not about having low self-esteem. It's perfectly normal to be afraid in certain situations like watching a scary movie or taking a ride on the world's largest rollercoaster, for example! Then of course there are fears that are phobias, like the fear of flying, fear of dogs, fear of crowds or small spaces. These fears are often so severe that professional help is the best route to take to deal with them effectively.

Then there are those fears that seem overwhelming but often can be dealt with without the need for a therapist. For example, you may have a fear of being laid off from your job because of the economy and you spend a lot of time worrying and afraid of being broke or losing your home. While this is a real fear, it isn't an insurmountable one.

Both fears that are phobias and fears that are not nearly as extreme can have a direct effect on your self-esteem. For our purposes, I'm focusing on everyday fears like public speaking, speaking up for yourself and trying new things in life.

In those cases, when you feel afraid to do what for others seems easy and effortless, your fear can be traced back to self-esteem. Those fears then take away your confidence to follow through.

The Solution

1. The key to overcoming your fears is to figure out if your fear is genuine or baseless. Here's an easy way to do that.

If for example you are afraid to speak in front of a group of people, ask yourself why you are afraid. Is there a logical reason to fear speaking in front of others? What's going to happen if you do? Will the sky fall? The point of this exercise is to help you recognize real fears from those you've created in your mind.

Let's say you are afraid to ask for a raise. Is there any sound reason you should not be asking for a raise?

Look at the facts.

For example:

Do you have an excellent track record with your company?

Is your current salary in line with others in your position?

Write down why you should get a raise and if the facts make sense then you know there's no reason to be afraid if you genuinely deserve a raise based on facts and you can back them up.

2. Face your fears head on! Often fears like trying new foods or traveling to foreign countries are all in your mind. These fears cause you to lose confidence in yourself.

Make a list of your fears, start with the small ones first. Then over time tackle each one by challenging yourself to face each one. Work your way up to your biggest fears. Tackling the small ones will give you the confidence to deal with bigger fears.

Are you obsessed with perfection? In the next section you'll learn why "being perfect" is not such a good thing after all.

Strategy 6: Perfection - How to Stop Trying to be Perfect

Is This You?

Do you constantly focus on making sure everything you do is perfect and get emotional if something doesn't quite measure up?

Are you known as an over achiever but you still feel like a failure?

Do you focus on the smallest of things in an attempt to make every little thing perfect?

The Issue

Perfection can be one of the biggest destroyers of both self-esteem and confidence. The mere idea of trying to create perfection means you will never achieve what you want in your life because mistakes happen. When someone spends their life seeking perfection and enjoys a stretch where everything "appears" perfect to them, it is emotionally devastating when that illusion of perfection is somehow damaged.

A perfectionist can also be a great example of someone with a lot of self-confidence, but low self-esteem.

A classic example of this is when you or someone you know grows up in an environment where failure is not looked upon favorably. At some point a false belief develops that makes you think everything has to be perfect. So you go about confidently doing things but at the same time are worried about failing constantly no matter how well you get things done. It's enough to drain all the fun out of your life!

The Solution

1. Focus on the fact that life is not perfect. There are ups and downs in everything we do. Instead of focusing on failing, focus on achievable goals. In other words, don't set the bar so high that the likelihood of failing is high.

2. Remember that who you are as a person is not determined by your successes or failures. When you fail at something, that's separate from who you are. Just because you lose a job, fail a class or lose a client doesn't mean you are a failure.

3. When you're working, playing a sport, taking care of your family and a long list of other everyday things, don't focus on little things that may not be working out as planned. Instead look at situations as a whole. It takes a lot of little parts to make one thing successful. By not focusing on the small stuff, you can enjoy more of what you have accomplished and appreciate it a lot more as well.

In the next and final section on self-esteem, I thought it would be important to mention the importance of positive self-esteem and children.

Strategy 7: Children - Raising Self-Esteem in Your Child

I wanted to mention just a few points in regards to children and self-esteem. So much of who we become as adults and how we see ourselves either positively or negatively is formed from a very early age.

Young Ears Hear More Than You Realize

It can be really easy to say things around children, especially if they are very young, and assume they are too young to really know what you're talking about. But the thing is, young minds are like sponges and they soak up information they hear and see every day even though you may not be aware of it.

Children Repeat What They Hear

I remember several years ago when one of my friend's sons who was about a year and a half at the time was starting to say words here and there. Often he would sit on the floor when my friend would have conversations on the phone. He would sit and play with his toys like any other toddler.

One day while playing alone, he picked up a toy phone and said "Hello?" He then went through a series of sounds with his voice that was all gibberish. Then he stopped and said "Okay bye talk to you later!"

All the time we thought he wasn't paying attention when she was on the phone, he was. He had learned from listening how to start the conversation, there's a lot of stuff going on in the middle and then when it's over you say "bye."

Now imagine if during those same conversations there were negative things being said. Just mentioning a child's name will make them listen more closely. Adding a negative comment about them routinely and eventually they will catch on. It happens a lot more than you may realize...like the mom or dad we've all seen screaming at their young child in the middle of a crowded store or restaurant.

So it's really important to choose your words wisely when speaking about your child. For example, don't say negative things about their looks even if you're just teasing and not meaning harm. It may be funny to you, but to a child you are the most important person in their world. They look up to you, they love you and want to please you. If you're making fun of them, imagine how they'll begin to feel about themselves. After all, you wouldn't lie to them right? So it must be true.

As your child gets older, don't say things like:

"You're lazy."

"You'll never be good enough."

"You're too fat. Stop eating so much!"

Statements like these can hurt, and if said often enough will make your child believe they are true and they may go into adulthood believing less of themselves.

Fears

Encourage young children to explore their environments. Take them to a children's museum where they can touch things and see things they've never seen before. This will help your child to not fear trying new things in life and ultimately lead a happier more confident life.

How Confident Are You?

Your confidence or lack thereof in yourself, others or your abilities to do something stems from low self-esteem. In the previous sections I shared some strategies you can use to rebuild your self-esteem.

In the next several sections I'm going to focus on more strategies, but these will be focused on rebuilding your self-confidence. But don't forget, self-esteem and confidence go hand and hand, so make sure you apply the relative strategies I've outlined if you want to become more confident.

How To Gauge Your Confidence Level

One of the best ways to determine your level of confidence is to gauge your comfort level in various situations. Remember the self-esteem questions and the importance of paying attention to how you feel and your body language?

The same exercise works for confidence too but I'd like you to try something a little different. In addition to answering the questions, either record yourself asking the questions with a video camera or just use a simple web cam. Then when you're done watch yourself on the video. Look for those "tells" we talked about in the section called "How's Your Self-Esteem?"

To take it one step further, talk about times and situations where you doubted yourself and didn't feel confident.

If you aren't able to record yourself, that's OK too. Just go through the exercises the same way that you did with the earlier set of questions.

Here's a list of questions you can use but feel free to expand wherever you feel compelled to do so. That will be further confirmation on an area of your life that needs more work.

1. Do you shy away from participating in new activities because you believe you're not smart enough to get the job done?

2. Do you constantly put yourself down in front of others?

3. Do you want to get out and enjoy more social activities but you get nervous and you're afraid to approach the opposite sex?

4. Do you want to have more fulfilling relationships but you just let others walk all over you?

5. Do you let unfounded fears stop you from meeting new people, advancing in your career and growing as a person?

Results

You will find that areas where your self-confidence wasn't where you would have liked correspond to areas where your self-esteem is low as well. This isn't true in every single instance, but for the most part you'll find this pattern to be pretty consistent.

For example, if you note that you're not very confident when it comes to taking on new projects at work, it may be due to your self-esteem issues dealing with fear or even your tendency to be a perfectionist.

If you've gone through the self-esteem exercises, you've gotten through the tough part. Remember the more you focus on making the necessary changes the sooner you'll enjoy more out of your life.

In the next sections, I'm going to give you some easy strategies you can use to start rebuilding your self-confidence starting today!

Strategies for Gaining Self-Confidence

Now it's time to take a look at some simple strategies you can use to build your self-confidence. Don't let the simplicity of each fool you. Gaining self-confidence doesn't require a lot of difficult tasks, but what it does require is persistence and consistency.

That's where a lot of people get tripped up when they're working on becoming more confident. Getting from where you are right now to where you want to be requires you to put in the effort on a daily basis until you begin to feel change taking place within you.

It's kind of like expecting to gain muscle without working out and eating a healthier diet.

So put in the time and effort and you'll see the results you want.

Here's what we'll cover:

Strategy 1: Self Image - Building Yourself up Confidently

Strategy 2: Relationships - How to be More Confident in Every Relationship

Strategy 3: Experience - How to Take Bad Experiences & Use Them to Build Your Confidence

Strategy 4: Faith - The Ultimate Confidence Builder!

Strategy 5: Self Talk - Create Your Own Personal Self Commercial to Keep Your Confidence Up

Strategy 6: Habit - How to Make Positive Self Confidence a Habit

Strategy 1: Self Image - Building Yourself Up Confidently

Self image issues can really cause problems with your confidence. It's amazing how making even small changes to your personal appearance or the way you see yourself can do wonders for your confidence.

Self Image Confidence Building Tips

1. Treat yourself to a new wardrobe or a few new outfits or suits. Buy what you enjoy wearing and not what others "think" you "should" be wearing.

When you wear clothes that make you feel good about yourself you automatically feel more confident. Think about the last time you wore a new dress, suit or whatever. How did you feel? If you love the way you look in something, what else happens? You walk more confidently because you feel great!

2. If you're not happy with your body then you've got to do something to change how you feel about your body. For most, that means diet and exercise. Trust me, after starting my own journey to lose more than 100 pounds, I am still amazed at how much better I feel about myself. I'm healthier, happier and a lot more confident. I know that even getting started down a path to increased health can have a huge effect on one's self image.

3. Stop comparing your body to others. It's self defeating and a waste of energy. Instead when you catch yourself doing that, stop and think about what you like about yourself. The more you do this, you'll eventually stop comparing yourself to others and learn to like yourself even more.

Strategy 2: Relationships - How to be More Confident in Every Relationship

Relationships, either in marriage or dating, can really test your confidence. If your relationships aren't as strong as you'd like them to be, take inventory of yourself first. It's so easy to blame the other person for everything, but the truth of the matter is if you're having issues in your relationship, whatever that is, it is a symptom of a bigger problem.

Relationships with family members and friends are also important and should be healthy and loving as well.

Low self-esteem can ruin relationships.

You can't control what someone else decides to do or say, but you can control what you do.

Relationship Confidence Building Tips

1. If your significant other is used to putting you down or making you feel unimportant it's time to change the rules! Let him or her know that if they want the relationship to last and thrive, you will no longer put up with demeaning behavior. Then you have got to be willing to follow through and don't give in to past behaviors.

2. Learn to be happy with or without him or her in your life. Your happiness should not depend on whether or not you have a husband or wife, boyfriend or girlfriend in your life. If you think you can't be happy unless you have someone in your life, that's a self-esteem issue that needs to be addressed. Once you realize that you can be happy on your own, you will be a lot more confident about a lot of things in your life. You will also enjoy better relationships as well. That's because when you show the world you can live your life happily on your own, you are showing just how confident you are in yourself.

3. Be sure to surround yourself with positive people you can form and maintain strong healthy relationships with. Do not tolerate anyone who thinks it's okay to put you down or do other things that work against your self-confidence. Be calm, but be firm and let them know what you will and what you won't put up with. Most people will respect that and act accordingly. If someone insists on being disrespectful, you don't have to get angry, simply don't engage them or the behavior and eventually they will remove themselves from your life.

How's that for rebuilding your confidence?

Strategy 3: Experience - How to Take Bad Experiences & Use Them to Build Your Confidence

Experiences, both good and bad, can work against you if you allow them to. It's all about acknowledging both for what they really are. Experiences are like classes in life. You can't learn about who you are and life in general unless you experience different things.

But if you allow the bad experiences to dominate your thinking then you will eventually do major damage to your self-confidence.

Experience - Confidence Building Tips

1. It's been said that we spend more time replaying a negative experience over and over in our minds than we spend thinking about positive experiences. Have you ever had an argument with someone in the morning but then spent the rest of the day thinking about it?

At those moments you are allowing a bad experience to dictate your happiness and sabotage your self confidence. To keep that from happening, when you catch yourself going back to that bad experience, change the movie going on inside your mind to something more positive. The more you do that the quicker you can move on. Sure that one time may not destroy your self-confidence, but we do things out of habit. If you don't change that habit, in the end you'll only do harm to yourself. You'll learn more about how you make building your self-confidence a habit in strategy 6: "Habit - How to Make Positive Self Confidence a Habit".

2. Look at every experience and ask yourself, "What did I learn from this and how can I improve upon it? This way you are not allowing a bad experience to root itself in your mind. You are making an active decision to control how you react. This will make you feel more confident about decisions and you will not fear outcomes. You will be mentally prepared.

3. Congratulate yourself when you do something well. If you experience getting a promotion, winning in some type of sport or successfully achieving something else, be proud of yourself. Don't talk about how you could have done even better if only I had (fill in the blank here). Just enjoy the success and be content that you did your best.

Strategy 4: Faith - The Ultimate Confidence Builder!

I could write an entire book on the subject of faith. When you have complete faith in something, your confidence level goes through the roof!

As I stated earlier, I am a Christian and my faith in God is unwavering. You have to ask yourself what drives you? Do you have enough faith in God? Yourself? Others in your life?

I think faith is the ultimate confidence builder because you have to believe deeply in something in order to have confidence that what you believe in will get you through anything in your life.

Faith - Confidence Building Tips

1. If your faith isn't as strong as you would like, then your confidence is most likely challenged as well. To rebuild confidence, you'll have to rebuild your faith.

People talk about having faith in God, their religion, loved ones and even the leaders of their country. But the fact is, before you can have unshakable faith in any of those, you must have the confidence to believe.

If you've neglected your religious practice take the necessary steps to realign yourself with your religious faith. Attend regular services and spend time with like-minded individuals who can help you get your confidence back.

2. If your faith in others has waned, reconnect with them and see if you can figure out what went wrong. Then make a commitment to repairing that relationship. Even if it doesn't work out the way you would like, your confidence will be stronger simply because you took steps to try.

3. Don't be afraid to express your faith. Whatever it is, it is a part of who you are as a person. When all else fails you can feel confident and comforted by your faith. Protect it, cherish it and allow it to help you enjoy life.

Strategy 5: Self Talk - Create Your Own Self Commercial to Keep Your Confidence Up

In business, especially if you're an entrepreneur, one of the first things you learn is the importance of creating your own "elevator speech." An elevator speech is one or two lines you memorize about yourself and whatever your business service provides when someone asks what you do for a living.

It should also sell you and make you stand out from the crowd.

Instead of saying, "Oh I uh. . . I sell real estate in Los Angeles...are you looking to buy?"

You might say this instead...

"I sell the most expensive real estate to some of the richest buyers in southern California!"

I don't think I have to ask which one sounds more interesting right?

Positive Self Talk Confidence Building Tips

1. To help you become more confident about yourself, create your own "elevator speech" about you as a person. Just write down what you feel are your best qualities and what your goals are in life. Then each morning before you start your day, look at yourself in the mirror, smile and recite your elevator speech to yourself.

Memorize it and any time you find you need a confidence boost, repeat your speech to yourself in your head.

It's important to make sure you smile. That's because just the act of smiling can release "happy endorphins" that make you feel good the longer you smile or laugh.

This technique can do wonders for your self-confidence and your self-esteem, so make it a new daily habit.

2. At the end of each day right before bed, repeat your elevator speech to yourself. By choosing to recite positive things about yourself right before sleep, you're setting the stage for a better night of sleep and a more motivating energized morning ahead.

Strategy 6: Habit - How to Make Positive Self Confidence a Habit

In the earlier section, How to Be Happier: A Blueprint for Creating More Joy In Your Life, I wrote about how happiness can be learned. When it comes to becoming more confident, I believe that can be learned as well.

I also think that once you have a plan in place to become more confident you can achieve your goal by making confidence a habit.

Think about it this way...how does a quarterback become good at what he does?

Well, let's see, he puts in a lot of practice, he studies the game, he plays the game.

But that's not all. He takes the time to learn specific techniques that allow him to throw the ball with more accuracy. Now here's where habit enters the picture. When an NFL quarterback is on the field and he's under pressure to get that ball thrown down field or risk getting sacked by the other team he has to make some very quick decisions.

He doesn't have time to stop and think about throwing drills and such. Instead he has to rely on habit. He throws the ball and scans the field out of habit so he can make quicker decisions.

Here's another example.

Have you ever driven home or to work and upon arriving at your final destination you realize you don't even remember making half the turns you normally make to get to work or home?

That's because you have driven the same route so many times that it has become habit. You don't have to pull out a map every time you drive to work each day and return home in the evening. Sure memory plays a role, but before you memorize something you develop a habit of doing something the same way over and over again.

Habit Confidence Building Tips

1. You can start creating new positive habits that will help you build and maintain strong confidence in yourself and in everything you do.

Make it a point to approach your everyday life with confidence. For example, challenge yourself. How many times have you gotten in an elevator where no one says anything to anyone else? It's amazing when you are in a tiny space and it's dead silent. Break the ice! Be bold and be confident. From now on, when those elevator doors open, smile and say "Good Morning!" Even if no one replies keep smiling! After you've done it a few times you'll actually look forward to it. The boost to your own self-confidence from such a seemingly small action will amaze you.

2. Make it a habit to be genuinely interested in someone else. Ask about their family and engage them on a personal level. When you stop focusing on yourself and show interest in others, it's not only good for your confidence it's great for your spirit too!

Increased Self-Confidence Will Make You Feel Unstoppable

You've learned about self-esteem and how it plays a direct role in your ability to be a lot more confident in your life. I've shared strategies for dealing with those self-esteem issues and steps to take to build your self-confidence as well.

If you spend time working on yourself consistently, you can make positive changes that will make you feel unstoppable!

Action Not Planning

It's easy to spend a lot of time reading about what you should do, but if you don't take action, you're not going to increase your confidence. I know it may seem tough in the beginning, but the fact that you picked up this book means you're ready to change. You're ready to take charge of your life and not waste any more of your valuable time watching the world pass you by. This is your time to experience your life with more confidence. With that you will create a happier version of yourself. If you have young children, they will reap the benefits too because they will do as you do.

Imagine this….

You get out and enjoy more of what life has to offer and you do so with a new level of confidence!

You enjoy stronger more loving relationships because you realize you bring a lot to the table and others respect you.

You live your life on your own terms and choose to lose weight because you want to and not because of what other think or say about you.

You embrace change and welcome new experiences because your self-esteem enhances your self-confidence and that makes you feel awesome!

You no longer focus on being perfect and instead you accept yourself as you are and that's good enough!

You are in control of your emotions and you are no longer overly sensitive.

You never let the opinions of others decide your happiness...you are happy and more confident in your own skin!

You can make the necessary changes to build your confidence and get more out of your life. You can do it...I'm rooting for you!

How to Be Positive: A Blueprint for Developing a Positive Attitude

Is Your Glass Half Full or Half Empty?

There's no doubt you've heard that saying at least a few times in your life, but have you ever stopped to think about it and answer the question? Your answer will theoretically provide clues as to how you see yourself and the world. Although a glass half full or half empty are essentially the same, the theory is if you choose half full then you are thought to be more positive and optimistic. If you choose half empty then the opposite would be true.

Now here's something that may surprise you. Most people have no idea whether or not their "glasses are half full or half empty" because most never really pay much attention to whether or not they're living life from a positive or pessimistic point of view. Really, who bothers to sit down and think about it, with so much going on in the world and the amount of constant distractions we have to deal with…things like television, the Internet, politics and keeping up with the lives of others via Facebook. Oh and let's not forget work, school, social events, keeping up with the kids and paying the bills. With all of that going on who has time to sit and wonder whether or not their attitude is positive right?

All of those "distractions" I just mentioned are reasons why you should focus on how you view yourself and the world.

Why?

Because your opinion of yourself and your outlook on others and the world can determine how well you live your life.

How Do You See The World?

Often the way we choose to see things whether from a positive point of view or a negative one, will almost always determine the outcome. Here's what I mean by that.

I have a good friend who is the perfect example of this. This guy has a big heart and would give you the shirt off his back if you needed it. The odd thing about him is that he is always expecting the worst. Here he is, this wonderfully nice person who's always ready to lend a helping hand, but at the same time he spends about 90% of his time being negative about everything.

I remember one beautiful sunny day, it was about 80 or 85 degrees and clear blue skies…just a picture perfect day. My friend said, "Well it's sunny now but it could all change in a blink of an eye!…the winds could get really violent and before you know it we're running for our lives from a tornado!" It doesn't matter to him that he lives in Los Angeles where the chances of a tornado whipping through the Southland is as about as likely as a snow free winter in Chicago!

My poor friend is the same way about everything. He got a great promotion at his job and a nice pay increase. That was 2 years ago and to this day he goes on and on about how he could lose his job at anytime.

Clearly my friend's glass is half empty.

Does your glass look like his?

Imagine how much happier my friend would be if he started to look at himself and the world from a more positive perspective. I admit, this example is a bit extreme, but I think you get the point. Something else to keep in mind is that negative thinking could also point to self-esteem issues. In the section of the book, How to Be Confident: A Blueprint for Increasing Your Self-Confidence, you read some clear examples that show how your view of yourself and the world around you can have an effect on your ability to be more positive or negative.

Now you don't have to be as extreme as my friend in order to be in need of a mindset tune-up. Here are a few examples and if any ring a bell with you, then it's time to take steps to work on your attitude and thinking.

*When faced with an obstacle, do you automatically assume it will be difficult or do you try to look at the bigger picture before you decide whether or not you can accomplish whatever it is you need do?

*Do you complain about something or someone regularly?

*Are you the life of the party or the person people tend to avoid?

*Do you start your day dreading going to work or do you more often recognize how lucky you are to have employment?

*Do you gossip about other people to anyone willing to listen or do you ignore rumors and remain silent?

When it comes to becoming more positive it's probably one of the best things you can do for yourself. It's not about walking around in a bubble thinking all is right with the world and nothing bad ever happens. Instead, it's about acknowledging the good things in your life and choosing to focus on those things.

Think of it this way…if you only had minutes left to live and were given the opportunity to spend your last minutes thinking about anything you wanted, would you really want to focus on something negative or something that made you smile and feel good?

In the next section, you'll learn how having a positive attitude can lead to great relationships, higher income, a happier life overall and even better health.

Your Attitude Does Affect Your Life

In the previous section I asked you to answer a few questions to help you identify whether your glass is half empty or half full. If you're being open and honest with yourself and you've identified some areas in need of improvement then congratulations! Pat yourself on the back! It takes a lot to admit you need to change. It can also be a bit scary even though it could benefit you immensely.

Change for a lot of people can be pretty uncomfortable. You may be very comfortable seeing your world or certain parts of it as a half empty glass, but I promise that if you're willing to make becoming more positive a commitment now, you'll live a happier more productive life later. Positive change begins with an adjustment to your attitude.

How Attitude Affects Your Life

My grandmother used to teach lessons about people and life in a very simple but effective way. See, anytime I or one of the kids in the neighborhood did something out of line, she would say "That kid needs an attitude adjustment!"

If I did something she didn't like, she would say the same thing to me. One summer when I was about 14, I finally got around to asking her what she meant by that. I mean I had heard her say it like a gazillion times but never really understood what she meant.

She simply smiled at me and said, "When someone goes around doing something or saying something that's inappropriate, it can be traced back to how they think about themselves and everyone else. It's about their attitude. If they are having a bad day then they need to adjust or change their attitude if they want to at least enjoy the rest of the day. If they are constantly running around causing problems for themselves and others, then they need to change the way they are thinking the majority of the time if they want to have a happier life."

From that point on, I would catch myself whenever I noticed my attitude was leaning on the negative side and as my grandmother always said, I would give my attitude an adjustment. It was and still is amazing how paying attention to your attitude can lead to better outcomes.

A Bad Attitude Can Keep You Broke, Alone, Unhappy, Sick & Tired!

Really?

Absolutely!

Let's take your job for example. You could be the sharpest pencil in the box, but if your attitude is always negative, do you really think management would be that enthusiastic about promoting you? If you and another both have the same abilities and education, but the other candidate has a much better or perceived to have a better positive attitude who is more likely to be promoted?

No one wants to spend 8 hours, 5 - 6 days a week listening to someone with a bad attitude. Plus it can be really bad for business especially if you work in customer service! If you maintain a consistently bad attitude you will put your career on hold. That also means you can limit the amount of money you earn. In severe cases, you can be fired for having a bad attitude no matter how great your work ethic may be.

If you're a business owner keep in mind that your bad attitude often has a trickle down effect, meaning that how you treat and speak of others can become the way your employees treat and speak to each other. An employee with a poor attitude will communicate that with current and potential customers and I can almost guarantee that your bottom line will suffer for this.

A positive attitude can have a tremendous effect! Co-workers are more willing to help you if your attitude is positive. Your supervisor is more likely to promote you or acknowledge your contributions. Having a more positive attitude towards your work can also boost your productivity. You'll notice your work projects improve greatly because when you're positive about what you are doing, you tend to be naturally more thorough and focused on giving your absolute best.

Relationships

All relationships…marriage, dating, business, family and friends can be strengthened or damaged beyond repair by your attitude. If your attitude is always negatively focused, you can almost set your clock as to how long that relationship is going to last. That doesn't mean your spouse, family member or friend will disappear out of your life. What it means is that the healthy relationship…the one that was fun and loving can fade. You may find some will avoid being around you at all costs.

Unfortunately, if your attitude is really bad, the one you love may leave. So when you're examining yourself and your attitude, think about whether or not the love and friendships you have are worth saving and nurturing.

Happiness & Health

Many studies have been done to determine how having a bad attitude can affect health. It has not been proven that a bad attitude makes you any more likely to suffer a major illness or die at an earlier age, however, walking around with a negative attitude can have a measurable effect on how you feel. Depression and emotional issues linked to a chemical imbalance are pretty common. Think about it…how can you be happy if you're always in bad attitude mood? It has to affect you physically even if it's minor. The next time you catch yourself having a negative storm as I like to call it, notice how you're sitting. Are you slumped over? Fists clenched? Biting your lower lip?

Can you see how your attitude can affect your ability to enjoy your life?

Attitudes Can Be Contagious

In the example about having a bad attitude in your work environment, I mentioned the "trickle down effect" that a bad attitude can have on a business. The same is true at home. Kids pick up habits from the ones they love the most...their parents. If you've got a poor attitude, in time your children will develop the same outlook on life. Just hanging around someone who is always speaking negatively can rub off on others. So it's really important to choose who you spend your time with wisely if maintaining a healthy positive perspective is important to you.

How To Check Your Attitude

Now that we've explored the consequences of a bad attitude it would be a good idea for you to take a look at your own attitude.

Here's why that's important to do...

Attitudes like a lot of other things we do as humans are so ingrained that we may not see ourselves as others do. It's easy to walk around assuming everything is great and your attitude is fine just the way it is.

Is This You?

*Do you complain about the food at almost every restaurant you visit?

*Do you go shopping and complain you can never find anything worth buying?

*Do you say things like, "Oh I bet they will be all out of my favorite (insert whatever here) by the time I get there!"

*Do you look for the bad in almost every situation?

*Do you expect to miss your flight even though you arrive to the airport 2 hours early?

*Do you say things like, "If I didn't have bad luck, I wouldn't have any luck at all?"

*How about this one, "I would buy a car from them but then they'll probably try to cheat me!"

Of course that's a very small sample but I'm sure you get the idea of where I'm going with this. If your attitude needs an adjustment, I have some strategies to help get your attitude in better shape.

Are you with me?

Great!

Next let's take a look at the power of thoughts and how thinking positively or negatively can open amazing doors or keep them shut!

Thoughts Have Power

Your thoughts, whether positive or negative, can have a profound effect on your life and the lives of others. Just think about that statement for a minute. Repeat it to yourself a few times and really let it sink in.

Almost everything you see, feel, hear and touch all existed as a thought first. The car you drive, the home you live in, the food you eat and even your favorite television show all came from thoughts. The songs you sing on the radio, the uplifting sermon you heard in church or that great idea you came up with all began from a thought. Unfortunately, the negative things we see and hear all begin with thought as well and the outcomes match accordingly. The biggest difference between thoughts formed from positive thoughts and from negative thoughts are the outcomes they produce.

Are you familiar with the saying, "Pick your poison?" It can be applied to your thoughts too. If you choose to focus on negative thinking most of the time, you are picking a mental poison that can create things in your life that you may not want. The outcomes or results of thinking negatively can create self-esteem issues in yourself and others. Negative thoughts can keep you from enjoying life. They can even keep you from achieving goals in your life.

When it comes to thoughts, you have the power to choose them one way or the other. That doesn't mean you can't switch things up. It's human nature to feel one way or the other depending on what's going on with you. Having a bad day that leads to some negative thinking is not likely to ruin your life or threaten your happiness long term. It is more about the kind of thinking that dominates your mind on a daily basis.

The Power of Positive Thought

To be clear, I'm not talking about you walking around for 24 hours a day only entertaining positive thoughts and only believing that all is perfect. That's not healthy. What I am talking about is paying closer attention to the way you choose to think. Here's something you can try right now to help you understand just how powerful positive thoughts can be.

Think about something that made you angry or disappointed you recently, or if you had a spat with someone over something and you're still a bit upset with him or her. If you're like most people you can almost replay whatever happened in your mind like a mental DVR.

How do you feel? Angry? Ticked off? Hurt? Keep thinking about the incident in question and this time I want you to smile. Nice big toothy grin! Keep smiling while you think about what happened for a few minutes. Don't stop smiling. Now think about all the good things that person has done for you. The times they made you laugh or got you out of a bind. No matter how small there is something positive you can find about a person.

Now how do you feel?

If I'm right, you may still be a bit peeved but it may not seem quite as bad.

Am I right?

There may even be some positive thoughts creeping in right about now. See how your feelings, your thoughts and even your body language can change? That's the power of positive thinking.

When you're in a challenging life situation, it can be easy to take a left onto Negative Street, but that's the time to focus all of your energy on looking for and thinking about something positive. Getting a scary diagnosis about your health won't be changed because you're thinking positively, but you may find you are able to cope better if you allow yourself to think about the possibilities of recovery and feeling better. Your positive thinking can also be of great comfort to loved ones around you.

Negative thoughts have the power to steal your joy and cause a lot of other problems in your life. Historically, negative thoughts about everything from politics to religion, race, class, and lots of other issues has served as a catalyst and a reason to do harm to others.

Environment

The power of thought gets magnified either positively or negatively when you are exposed to a certain way of thinking day in and day out. If you are surrounded by friends and family who are generally positive, you are more likely to think in much the same way. On the other hand, if you are hanging around individuals who are negative most of the time, eventually their way of thinking is going to rub off on you too. It's human nature to become most like the ones who have the strongest influence on us.

I believe this is why teenagers who end up going down the wrong path early in life do so much of the time…because of the influence (thoughts) of others they look up to. Usually these are other teens that seem smarter and wiser and make parents seem out of touch and uncool.

What You Think About The Most Becomes YOUR Reality

If you spend the majority of time thinking about how great your life is and how excited you are about your future, you are more likely to enjoy success in many areas of your life. If something in your life doesn't go as planned, but you choose to look for the positives in the situations and see where improvements can be made, you are again more likely to succeed the next time around. Or you may decide a change of course is the way to go and move forward regardless of setbacks. Positive thinkers don't allow themselves to sit and feel sorry for themselves. Instead they figure out where they made their mistakes and try again.

Negative thinkers look for things to complain about all the time. If you would rather sit and come up with a laundry list of all the bad things that could go wrong, you are more likely to either not complete something or never even try. That's because your negative thoughts are so powerful, they can keep you from enjoying more in your life. Instead of going to a fun social event for example, negative thinkers will "think themselves" to a lonely night at home because they think it will be a waste of their time to go. They may say something like, "What's the point..I never meet anybody interesting anyway!" With that way of thinking, they're right...they won't...because they will stay home...alone.

By now you have an understanding of just how empowering and disabling your thoughts can be, but all is not lost you can learn to be more positive.

Just like most things in life you want to achieve, you're going to need a plan...you need strategies to help you become more positive in your thinking, your approach to life and to those you love and care for.

Strategies for Developing a Positive Mindset

The Plan

You should be very proud of yourself to be willing to focus on change in your life. It says a lot about you as a person. It shows you have integrity. It shows you care how others see you, but more importantly it shows the level of importance you place on improving yourself. After all, you can't be of help to anyone else in your life if you're not willing to work on yourself first.

As I mentioned in the last section, you have to have a plan in place. Just waking up one day and saying you're going to be more positive is not enough. You also need to have a clear reason as to why you want to change.

Find Your Motivation

One way to figure out why you want to change is to look at your life and ask yourself what you may lose if you don't change your outlook or thinking? Humans fear losing something more than they fear not having something in the first place.

Do you fear losing your job?
A relationship?
Old friends?

Figure out why you want to change and let that be the force that drives you to becoming a more positive person.

Strategies You Can Use

In the next sections, I've included some strategies that will help you to become more positive. Just remember, at the end of the day, if you don't put them to use in your daily life consistently then don't expect much in the way of positive changes. Consistency and persistence are the keys to enjoying a positive mind and a healthier life overall.

Here are the strategies we'll cover...

1. The 30 Day Challenge: How to Be More Positive One Day at a Time

2. Spying on Your Own Thoughts to Create Positive Changes

3. The Positive Power of Saying Thank You

4. Positive Affirmations

5. Turn the Television Off!

6. Immerse Yourself in Positivity

7. Get Your Exercise and Change How You Feel About Your Body

8. Prayer & Meditation: A One Two Punch to Knock Negativity Right Outta Your Life!

Now, let's get started!

Strategy 1: The 30 Day Challenge: How to Be More Positive One Day at a Time

What if I told you that in about 30 days from today you could be a happier more positive person? Would you be willing to give it a try? How badly do you want to change?

The 30 Day Positive Thinking Challenge

There was a study several years ago that stated it takes 21 days to change any habit. Since then many researchers disagree with that. In any case, what is in agreement when trying to promote change within yourself is consistency. My 30 day challenge is something I use in my own life when I want to focus on changing something that isn't working (a bad habit) or adding a new, positive habit.

I'm not here to say it's going to be a walk in the park. You know what they say, "If change was that easy then everyone would be doing it!" It will require discipline on your part. I can give you the tools but it's up to you to follow through.

The Challenge

For the next 30 days you're going to pick an area in your life you want to change that will allow you to open the door to more positive thinking. For example, if you complain about everything and everyone all the time, you will spend the next 30 days in a complaint free mode of thinking. That may sound extreme, but if your current thoughts are focused on complaining all the time, those are extreme negative thoughts you need to tame.

So in this case, when you begin to complain about something, stop yourself and ask if it's really necessary to complain about whatever it is and instead start looking for a way to solve whatever it is you're complaining about if possible. If it is something within your power to fix, why not do that instead of complaining about it to anyone that will listen? If it's something beyond your control, then ask yourself why you're giving it so much energy in your life?

When you stop and question yourself about what you are thinking it forces you to stop your old ways of thinking and adopt new ones.

Here's another example. If you love to gossip, challenge yourself to stop spreading rumors or even engaging in gossip with others for 30 days. The next time you get the urge to run to your favorite gossip buddy…stop! Ask yourself, would you want others speaking about your personal or work life behind your back? How would you feel if you were the subject of rumors that were untrue? Then challenge yourself to not take whatever you heard any further. Often people who approach you with the latest gossip do so because you have created a reputation of someone who will listen and spread the rumor. They come to you because they can count on you for that. It also makes you someone others don't confide in either because they know you will spread rumors and can't be trusted with sensitive information.

So instead of spreading gossip, challenge yourself to just walk away when you see the conversation is taking a negative turn. Refuse to get involved and the next time someone says something negative about someone, find something positive to say and walk away.

Example: a co-worker comes up to you and wants to share the latest gossip about your boss. You could say, "Well if that's true it's unfortunate and I hope everything works out for her." Turning the tables on negative gossip has a way of shutting down the conversation quickly. Try it and see what happens.

Stay Committed & The Results Will Speak For Themselves

The more you focus on change, the bigger the reward at the end. If you stick with it for the full 30 days, I guarantee you will feel and think differently. Thinking positively about something will start to feel more natural. In the beginning you may struggle a bit, it's okay that's to be expected but you have to be willing to correct yourself each time.

What To Do If You Slip Up

Change can be one of the hardest things to do. Especially when it comes to changing how you think about things. If you're a negative thinker, your habit of thinking that way has literally become hard wired into your mindset. It's going to take time to "rewire your thinking" and create change long term. So if you find yourself falling back into your old ways of thinking, the best thing to do is to acknowledge it and adjust your thoughts right then and there.

It's a lot like trying to discipline a child. Your thoughts can be like children with bad manners. It's up to you to be willing to correct yourself by guiding your thoughts to a more positive place instead. Do this every time and soon you will find you won't automatically begin to think negatively and instead you will look for a more positive solution. So don't beat yourself up if you slip…just adjust and keep moving forward.

Putting The Plan Into Motion

In the remaining sections on strategies, you can use the 30 Day Challenge plan for those as well. It's all about developing new positive ways of thinking. So decide which strategy you want to try and simply apply it to the 30 Day Challenge as outlined above.

Ready?

Here we go….

Strategy 2: Spying on Your Own Thoughts to Create Positive Changes

Thinking about things a certain way can change your life in many different ways. Sometimes, you may be so caught up in life stuff in general that you may not even be aware of your thoughts and how they may be affecting your life.

Take a notebook and begin "spying" on your own thoughts. In this case, spying means writing down what you catch yourself thinking about throughout the day. Not stuff like taking out the garbage and picking up groceries at the store. Instead, pay attention to the thoughts that typically follow other thoughts.

For example, if you remember you need to pick up groceries at your local supermarket but then follow that thought up with, "It's going to be crowded I just know it!" Write that thought down. Then immediately write down a new thought to replace the negative one.

For example, "I need to pick up groceries at the supermarket, there's always a lot of people shopping there maybe I'll run into an old friend while I'm there!" The whole point is to do this every time so you can train your thoughts to stop looking for negative stuff.

Apply this simple thought spying technique using the 30 Day Challenge and if you commit yourself to the full 30 days you're going to be amazed at how much you change and how differently you'll feel about yourself.

Strategy 3: The Positive Power of Saying Thank You

When was the last time you said "thank you" for something you use every single day of your life? We all walk around taking a lot of what we have for granted. That doesn't mean you're a bad person. It's easy to not think about what you have until you lose it. That's when most people realize how fortunate it was to have something or someone in their life…after it's gone.

Being thankful each day is a wonderful way to not only become more positive in your thinking and in your life, but it will also make you a lot more patient and compassionate for others.

The Plan

Remember you can use The 30 Day Challenge for this strategy. I can tell you from my own experience, this daily exercise of saying "thank you" will have an amazing effect on you. Get yourself a notebook or journal. Each day you're going to write down something you're thankful for in your life. There are no right or wrongs here, so don't worry about choosing only certain things.

Here are some examples:

*I'm thankful for my vision.
*I'm thankful for my ability to walk.
*I'm thankful for my family.

Taking Gratitude A Step Further

I know everything in life isn't so simple. So if you have something in your life that is a major source of negativity like a job you don't like, you may want to think about using the 30 Day Challenge to change the way you think about your job, your position and the company you're working for. If you don't, you may run the risk of losing your job. For many, that is not an option.

Instead of complaining about your job, focus on the positives. Each day for the next 30 days find something positive about your job and let that be your positive thought for the day.

Here's an example:

"I am thankful I have employment because there are so many people who can't even find a job, yet I have one. It may not be perfect but I'm thankful it pays me so I can feed my family."

On another day you might say:

"I am thankful I have this position. If I apply myself and stay positive I could move up, get a promotion and make more money!"

Can you see where this is going? Can you imagine how much differently you're going to feel about your job 30 days from now? You may decide it's not such a bad job after all, or your new way of thinking could give you the confidence to look for better employment elsewhere instead of complaining about the job you have.

Strategy 4: Positive Affirmations

There's a lot to be said about the power of thinking positively. Even more so, is the power of positive affirmations. Basically, affirmations are thoughts you can either say to yourself, out loud or even by writing them down that focus on positive changes in your life. There are also prerecorded affirmations you can purchase from places like Amazon.com for example.

Affirmations are not some magic thingy that will change your life overnight. They are literally new thoughts you repeat over and over again until the change you're trying to create becomes a reality.

You should also keep in mind that affirmations don't work for everyone. I think it's because it can be easy to write an affirmation that is so far from what you truly believe that you end up setting yourself up for failure right from the start. If the affirmations you're writing aren't really believable, your mind will automatically reject the new thoughts.

Examples of Good Positive Affirmations

"I enjoy talking with my coworkers and only speak positively when doing so."

"I enjoy eating healthy because I lose weight and feel better each day."

"I am making better financial decisions each day."

Examples of Not So Good Positive Affirmations

"I will never speak negatively about anyone ever again in my life!" (Nice thought but that may prove to be a bit tough)

"I can eat whatever I want and still lose weight!" (Good luck with that one!)

"I am going to win the lottery and all my bills will be paid! YAY!" (Sigh)

The obvious point is to make your affirmations simple, but most of all believable. You can focus on more than one subject matter each day, but you may have better results if you focus on one particular area of life first.

Strategy 5: Turn the Television Off!

For the next 30 days, take steps to take a break from things you have control over that typically lead you to negative thinking or habits.

Here are a few ideas:

1. This one will be tough if you love watching television. Stop watching tv for 30 days. You may be thinking what does television have to do with the way you think? Well think about the kind of stuff you see on tv each day.

Mornings

The morning news, rarely has anything positive to report. Instead most morning news programs can't wait to tell you how many crimes were committed while you were sleeping? Then there's bad news about the economy, murders, global warming and a long list of negative stories. Typically if there is any positive news to report they'll tell you at the end of the broadcast in about :10 seconds or less! Gee what a way to start your day huh?

After Work

After a long day at work you turn on the TV and get to watch crime drama after crime drama all featuring gruesome depictions of all kinds of murders. If you work at night you can watch reality judge shows or soap operas about crimes, bad relationships and tons of other negatively focused topics.

Right Before Bedtime

You get to fall asleep watching and absorbing stories about fires and mayhem not just in your city but from all over the world! Going to sleep night after night with all of that negative information literally embedded into your subconscious mind is a recipe on how to create daily negativity in your life.

You really won't realize how much power the constant negative news and various TV shows have on you until you stop watching for a month. If you find yourself slipping and you want to watch some television during those 30 days. Ask yourself what positive purpose will you gain from doing so. You may find that's a powerful enough thought to make you keep your focus away from watching TV.

What To Do Instead of Watching TV

How about learning a new language?

Read books and learn something new

Get out and exercise more

Get back to some old hobby you've neglected or start a new one

What To Expect After 30 Days

Your results are going to be different from someone else's but generally you may notice you're thinking a lot more clearly. You may also find that have the 30 days are up, your interest in watching television has decreased considerably or completely. You'll be more productive and discover things about yourself and others you never noticed before when the noisy distraction of television was in your way.

If you should decide to go back to watching TV after the 30 days, commit to watching specific programs that are positive and uplifting and limit the amount of time you watch each day or week.

Strategy 6: Immerse Yourself in Positivity!

When someone wants to learn a new language, the best way to achieve fluency is to immerse yourself into the language and culture as much as possible. You could use the same technique when it comes to changing the way you think.

Avoid Negative People!

This strategy may require a lot more discipline. You're going to do your best to stay away from individuals who contribute to your negative thinking. That may mean not hanging out with them as much as you do now. It may mean changing the subject every time they start getting negative. It could also mean not hanging around them at all!

For 30 days, seek out individuals who are positively focused. I enjoy fellowship with other Christians, as it is a very positive environment. Start going out more and meet new people that are more positive and fun to be around.

Read Positive Books

When you read, you open your mind up to learning new things. The library and bookstores have thousands of books written on the subject of becoming more positive. There are literally thousands of books about thinking positively. Probably one of the most famous is The Power of Positive Thinking by Dr. Norman Vincent Peale.

There are also tons of religious books in addition to the Bible you can read to keep your mind focused positively.

Write!

You can use a simple notebook to write down all the positive things going on in your life and you write positive expectations about your future as well. Then whenever you find yourself struggling to stay focused on the positives, you can refer back to your notebook and read thoughts that can help you recharge your positive spirit!

Strategy 7: Get Your Exercise and Change How You Feel About Your Body

If you have a negative self image because you're overweight, making the choice to exercise and change your eating habits can change the way you feel about yourself. I can relate firsthand. Before I decided to do something about my weight, I had a very negative feeling about my body, but once I decided to make better choices, I eventually lost 100 lbs! You can read how I did it in my series "How to Lose 100 Pounds" if this is something that you also struggle with.

The 30 Day Challenge is tailor made for getting your mind and thoughts about your body into a healthier positive frame of mind. You will not lose 100 lbs in 30 days! How much you do lose is going to be determined by your eating and exercise plan.

For 30 days you're going to eat healthier and get some kind of exercise each day. To help keep you motivated, think about the positive results you'll get to enjoy at the end of the 30 days. In fact, on days when you want to give up, think about the weight you'll lose if you stick with it. Think about how much better you'll feel about yourself and your body.

Then at the end of the 30 days you may decide to repeat the process. That's fine but at some point you'll want to think about applying some long term strategies to lose additional weight if you need to. The 30 Day Challenge is a great way to get your body and mind used to exercise and diet so when you're ready to go to the next level you will be a lot more positive about doing so because you'll have a whole month of success under your belt already!

Strategy 8: Prayer & Meditation

The power of prayer and meditation is a powerful one two punch when it comes to creating and maintaining a positive outlook. Researchers don't understand why prayer and meditation seems to have almost miraculous results for the people who practice them regularly. While it may be a mystery to science, if you have faith in what you believe in, it's not a mystery at all.

Prayer and meditation allows you to dismiss the negatives at the end of your day or to pave the way for a positive day ahead before you start your day. Millions of people all over the world make prayer and meditation the most important part of their day.

It is an opportunity to allow faith to help them steer away from negative thoughts. The more you pray and meditate, you may find that you have a level of peace within that can't be measured or even explained, so there's no need to participate in negative talk or actions. A mind that is at peace continues to seek and connect with peace and positivity.

Connect With Your Faith

Whether you're a Christian as I am or Jewish, Muslim or whatever spiritual path you've chosen, join in fellowship with like-minded individuals for regular prayer and worship. It's been said that prayer is talking to God and meditation is listening to God.

Take the next 30 days and make a promise to start and end your day with prayer and meditation. You'll be amazed at how positive you will begin to feel about yourself, your life and everything else.

Feed your soul with prayer and meditation and you will enjoy life from a perspective you never knew was possible.

Developing a Positive Attitude Can Lead to Big Change

I've shared the importance of thinking positively, the benefits of keeping a watchful eye on your attitude and strategies you can begin using right now to change your thinking for the better. You have the tools to work with, it's now up to you to put them to good use.

It may seem like a lot, and it may take you 2 or 3 times to make it all the way through The 30 Day Challenge, but if you give it your all, it will all work out and you will reap the benefits of engaging in positive thought.

Just hang in there and don't give up! You don't create major changes in your life by quitting. You create change by committing yourself to the goals you've set. Practice making your thoughts a priority in your life and you'll wonder what took you so long to figure it all out!

Remember, change is a journey with all kinds of lessons to learn along the way. Embrace them, learn from them, and be thankful every day.

How to Be Relaxed: A Blueprint for Reducing Stress in Your Life

Typical Situations That Can Cause Stress

There are so many things that contribute to a high level of stress in our everyday lives. Unfortunately, many of us don't even realize just how much stress we are under until we break down mentally, emotionally or physically. That's when we realize we need to find ways to lower our stress levels and relax.

In the next section, you'll learn more in detail about the effects of stress on your life but first take a look at the following examples of situations that cause stress and see if any ring a bell with you.

Money!

Worrying about not having enough money to pay bills and survive is the number one cause of stress. Other money related issues include worrying about not having enough money for retirement, a child's college education, buying a new home, paying a mortgage etc... What is also interesting is that if a person is used to not having money, they still worry about losing what money they do have. Stressing out over finances is not limited to the lack of money. Those who are considered rich might stress out about making the wrong investments and worry about being taken advantage of because of their wealth.

Health

In general, if you're like most people, you don't get stressed out over your health until your health becomes compromised in some way. For example, if you've smoked cigarettes for several years, you most likely do so without giving it much of a second thought. But if one day you are diagnosed with a disease or condition that changes your everyday life or could possibly be life threatening because of your smoking habit, then you worry and begin to experience an increased amount of stress.

Family Issues

Family problems can cause a lot of stress that seems to have a snowball effect. Here's what I mean by that. Let's say you and your spouse are having marital problems. It doesn't matter if it's about money, infidelity or something else. If it's big enough to cause constant bickering and an overall disconnect, it can cause undo stress to not just you and your spouse, but to your children as well. Even if your children aren't old enough to understand what's going on, the negative energy that stress can create can be "picked up" by other members of your family.

That's where the snowball effect I mentioned earlier comes in. Before you know it everyone in the house is stressed out and picking arguments with each other or doing all they can to avoid having any communication whatsoever.

If you are separating or getting a divorce, that's a major source of stress that can get out of control very quickly due to the strong emotions involved. Multiply that by 10 if you have children.

New Events In Life

Having a baby, getting a brand new job or moving to a cool new city should be happy occasions and for the most part they usually are, but just the thought of going into the unknown can be extremely stressful. For example, taking a new job in a city where you've never lived or visited is very stressful. You can spend a lot time worrying about whether or not you're making the right decision or whether or not you should stay at your current job.

Job Loss

Losing your job can create a lot of stress mainly because of the fear of what could happen if you don't find another job quickly enough. The stress from the loss of the job turns into stress worrying about finances and the possibility of losing your home and other possessions.

Even if losing a job is not an issue, there can be problems at your place of employment that can lead to stress. These might include problems with coworkers or supervisors. If you're in management it can be stressful trying to supervise a staff and be solely responsible for the productivity of your entire department. If you experience harassment on the job, that can lead to stress as well. Working long hours day in and day out can also create a lot of unwanted stress in your life.

Death of A Friend Or Loved One

Losing someone close to you can create dangerous levels of stress. Unlike other stresses in our lives, the death of a loved one is final and can't be changed. The grieving process can go on for an extended amount of time for some and that also extends the level of stress in a person's life.

I want to also include losing a beloved pet here. If you are a lover of dogs or cats or some other pet, they are often considered "one of the family" and losing them can be just as stressful.

Caring For Aging Parents

Most adult children will at some point find themselves becoming caregivers to their aging parents. It can be very stressful trying to take care of your parents and their needs while trying to balance various things within your own life at the same time.

Stress From Alcohol & Drugs

Excessive use of alcohol and drugs is dangerous and a major cause for stress that can be deadly.

The Effects of Stress

In the last section we took a look at some of the most common situations that can cause stress. Before you can begin to learn how to relax, it's important to understand the effect that too much stress can have on you.

How Your Body Responds To Stress

We all have something called the "fight or flight" response hard-coded into our DNA. You could say it is a built-in alarm system that alerts us to either confront something or someone that is threatening in some way or to run away from the threat. It occurs as a way to respond to a high level of stress taking place during a specific event.

Here's an example.

Let's say you're in a restaurant and a disagreement between two patrons ensues. What happens next is the result of an elevation in stress levels which causes the "fight or flight" response to kick in. What's even more interesting is that men are more likely to fight whereas women are more likely to take flight or at the very least try to calm the situation down before it escalates further. Of course that's not always the case but generally speaking that scenario is the most common. A woman is more likely to fight if she perceives her child, for example, is in some kind of imminent danger.

The fight or flight response can happen several times a day as it doesn't require something as dramatic as a loud physical confrontation. Whenever you are faced with a decision that causes you stress, your fight or flight response will kick in. Now that doesn't mean you're going to beat your boss up the next time she confronts you about your work performance. It simply means you will respond in a way that makes you feel you need to confront (fight) or perhaps deny (flight) depending on what the situation might be.

Stress of this nature can have a devastating effect on someone with heart problems. Many heart attacks take place after high levels of stress. So let's talk about how stress can affect your heart.

The Heart

Cardiologist use "stress tests" to check the health of your heart. By subjecting your heart to elevated levels of stress they can determine how much your heart can handle before something adverse occurs. The heart is very sensitive to stress, even when it's something as joyful as walking across the stage to accept your diploma. Having a baby or even watching someone have a baby can also be very stressful. When under stress your heart rate increases, your blood pressure can rise and your arteries can narrow. Prolonged stress can result in a heart attack or stroke.

Stress Can Cause Weight Gain

When I was 100+ lbs heavier, I seemed to often feel stressed out. Being overweight and suffering from some self-esteem issues can cause a lot of worrying and stress almost on a daily basis. For me, getting healthier and losing weight has had an amazing effect on my overall quality of life. (If weight issues are something you can relate to, you can check out my series of books called "How to Lose 100 Pounds" at the end of this book)

Researchers have found a link between weight gain and stress. It's a chemical in our bodies called cortisol. It's very common to lose your appetite when you're under an increased amount of stress, however, when your appetite returns your body goes into survival mode. Your body is programmed to survive by whatever means necessary. So after not eating for a period of time and your appetite returns cortisol is released to get you to eat food to replace nutrients and energy. The problem is that in some people cortisol levels remain high even after the stress you're under subsides. The elevated levels will cause you to eat more food and this could eventually lead to weight gain.

Carrying too much weight can also create stress on your heart because it has to work a lot harder. Your weight can also put stress on your joints making something as simple as walking a very painful event.

Digestive Disorders

Irritable bowel syndrome or IBS can be caused by prolonged periods of stress. This is because stress can cause indigestion, gas and constipation.

Women & Stress

Stress can cause miscarriages and can interfere with the menstrual cycle. This can lead to painful periods or periods that are longer or shorter than usual. Increased stress can also stop the menstrual cycle altogether.

Muscular Pain

Your body can manifest stress with sore stiff muscles which could lead to other problems like chronic back pain, headaches and sleeping problems.

Mental

Long periods of increased stress can cause major behavioral problems. You might find yourself snapping at others or reacting angrily about minor things. If left unchecked you could end up fighting depression. Constant worry about things going on in your life can cause emotional problems that can get worse over time. Not everyone responds to stress the same way. If you or someone you know tends to shut down when stress levels are elevated, seek professional help. A therapist can give you coping skills to help you deal with whatever is going on in your life. Shutting down and internalizing your stress will only make a bad situation a lot worse.

Skin Disorders

If you have skin disorders like acne or eczema, they can flair up during times of prolonged stress. When you're under a lot of stress your immune system is weakened and it can't do its job efficiently. Your immune system works to keep you healthy by attacking viruses and other foreign agents that enter your body. If you are experiencing a lot of stress, over time your immune system can literally break down. In addition to more intense flare-ups, stress can inhibit your ability to heal if you've been injured or your body is attempting to heal after a surgery.

Stress & Recovery

Cancer patients are routinely advised to engage in activities that can help them reduce the amount of stress they are under. Doctors are aware of the effects stress can have on any patient who is recovering from cancer treatments. Since their immune systems are compromised due to treatments like chemotherapy, it is extremely important to reduce stress as much as possible to minimize the effect that it can have on the patient's ability to heal.

Relationships

Stress can destroy relationships with your spouse, your family members, friends and coworkers. When you've got too much stress in your life, your ability to think clearly and make sound decisions can cloud your judgment and this can lead to divorce, broken friendships and other misunderstandings.

You Can Learn How to Relax

There are physical and mental things that you can do and learn that will greatly reduce the level of stress you're experiencing.

Now that you know all the damage stress can cause in your life, I'm willing to bet that you're ready to take steps to reduce this in your own life. You can lower your negative stress responses and learn how to relax your mind and your body.

I'll share some detailed relaxation strategies in the next sections, but don't skip ahead just yet. It's important to understand that relaxation is a state of mind that can be learned. Once you learn how to relax your mind, your body will follow. There is a mind/body connection that we all have that is very important to be aware of.

If your mind is filled with constant thoughts of worrying about finances, work, family matters and your health for example, your body will respond in any number of different ways. Refer back to the section on The Effects of Stress to refresh your memory. At this point in your life you may have learned to respond to stress in a way that causes other problems like headaches, back aches, heart and blood pressure problems and a lot more.

Learning How To Relax

It may sound odd that you need to learn how to relax...after all you already know how to do that right? Relaxing for most of us means getting home after a long day at work, kicking off our shoes and watching whatever is on television. Or maybe you take a vacation and spend a week in some exotic location. Both sound relaxing enough right?

Well let's take a look at each one.

In the example of relaxing in front of the television after a long day, this really isn't relieving stress. It is simply distracting your mind for a short period of time. Once your programs have ended you'll find your worrying thoughts return in full force.

What about that wonderful vacation?

Sure you can have a great time, but how many times have you or someone you know made the statement, "We had to come back from vacation so we could finally get some rest!" It sounds funny but there is some truth to that. Often when we go on vacation we end up ripping and running from one thing to the next almost nonstop in an attempt to see and do as much as we can. By the time our "relaxing vacation" comes to an end, we can't wait to get some sleep and rest!

So really, it's not that you can't relax, you just might not know how.

That is until now…

Relaxation Strategies To Help Reduce Stress

Now we get to the fun part! Coming up in the next several sections you're going to learn some simple but powerful strategies to teach you how to relax.

Here are the strategies covered:

1. Prayer & Meditation
2. Exercise
3. Music
4. Reading
5. Spa Day
6. Yoga
7. Hypnotherapy
8. Get A Hobby!
9. Fun Social Events

10. Pets
11. Aquariums
12. Regular Massage
13. Therapy And Support Groups
14. Take A Real Vacation
15. Unplug!
16. Get Your Sleep!
17. Diet
18. Visualization
19. Breathing Exercises
20. Have A Cup of Tea
21. Aromatherapy
22. Count to 10
23. Lay Off The Caffeine
24. Deal With The Issues That Are Stressing You Out

Let's take a look at each one by one and see how you can use each simple strategy to control stress and learn how to relax.

Strategy 1: Prayer & Meditation

Prayer

As a Christian I can vouch for the power of prayer in my life. When life's stresses sneak up on me, I turn to prayer to calm my nerves and ease my fears or worry. Prayer allows me to hand over my problems to God and clear my mind from worry.

If you are a Christian or are of another faith where prayer is a part of your religious practice, include prayer as a regular part of your day and you'll find your mind becomes more relaxed each day.

Meditation

The art of meditation comes in many forms but all can help you achieve high levels of relaxation you may have never experienced before. Researchers believe meditation can help patients heal faster when dealing with the effects of various invasive forms of treatment for several different life threatening diseases.

You may think meditation is too difficult to learn but actually there are many different ways to meditate. Some methods are as simple as breathing a certain way or very complex techniques that can only be learned after several years of practice. (You'll find a very easy deep breathing meditation in Strategy # 19 Breathing Exercises.)

Teaching you how to meditate goes beyond the scope of this book, so here are a few ideas to help point you in the right direction.

1. Check out books and DVDs at your local library to learn basic meditation techniques.

2. If you belong to a health club or live near a YMCA call and ask about meditation classes.

3. Check your local classifieds for group meditation classes in your area.

4. You'll also find tons of books on meditation on Amazon.com.

Strategy 2: Exercise

Lose Weight & Relax Your Mind At The Same Time

You already know the importance of exercising to lose weight and strengthen your body. Regular exercise also releases "feel good" hormones throughout your body. If you make exercise a regular part of your everyday life, you'll soon notice you are able to deal with the stresses of life a lot better.

If you've never exercised before, check out my book Exercising For Weight Loss for some ways to get started and stay motivated.

At the end of the day, exercise won't help you if you don't plan to take action.

Once you're working out regularly you'll begin to reap the benefits of exercise in no time.

1. Less anxiety

2. Clear thinking

3. Improved health

4. Control your stress

5. Enjoy natural relaxation

Strategy 3: Music

Music Can Soothe Your Soul & Relax Your Mind

Certain genres of music have been used to lower anxiety, create optimum learning environments, ease the fears of young children afraid of the dark and to relax the mind.

Music can help you relax before meditation, prayer and yoga. There are music collections recorded specifically to help the brain focus and relax.

Here are a few ideas of how you can use music to relax your mind and kick stress to the curb.

1. Listen to soothing music right before practicing meditation to relax your mind and body.

2. You can also listen to music while you are meditating if you find it doesn't distract you.

3. During times of stress listening to music you find positive and uplifting can help you relax before starting or ending your day.

4. Explore Classical music and you may find it is perfect for putting you in a better frame of mind.

Routine

You can train your mind to relax whenever there is an introduction to music. Each time you need to quiet your mind and relax tell yourself to relax. You may find this technique is more effective if you choose the same piece of music each time. In time it will become a "mental cue" similar to techniques used in hypnotherapy to get your mind to quiet random worrying thoughts and allow you to relax.

Salt Baths and Music

Try listening to music while soaking in a hot salt bath. If you do this 15-20 minutes right before bed, you might find that it can lead to a full night of comforting relaxing sleep.

Strategy 4: Reading

Reading Can Be Great For Relaxing Your Mind

Sitting down in a comfortable area where you won't be disturbed with a favorite book can give your mind a much needed break. It's important, however, to choose something that won't cause more stress. In other words, if you're stressed out because of problems in your marriage reading a novel about infidelity is not going to relax you at all. If anything it will make your own problems seem much worse.

Choose books that are positive, or even better, books that may help you deal with your stress. Think about books that make you smile, or give you confidence or make you feel good about yourself and life in general. By spending time reading books that pick up your spirits, you'll find yourself looking at your own issues from a slightly different perspective.

Strategy 5: Spa Day

Book A Day At The Spa!

Pampering yourself is a great way to help you manage stress and relax. So why not treat yourself to a day at the spa! A day spa would be a great idea and you can even invite your close friends to come along as well. Spending a day getting pampered is the ultimate stress reliever.

If you've never had the pleasure of spending time at a spa you're in for quite a treat. You can look for day spas in your area online or in your local phone book. Try booking your day during the week instead of on the weekends when the rates are much higher and spas tend to be the busiest.

If you book on a typically slow day of the week you'll enjoy a much quieter atmosphere and you'll have the full attention of staff.

Spa Services

Every spa has its own unique set of services but generally you can expect:

1. Massages

2. Manicures & Pedicures

3. Hot rock therapy

4. Body scrubs

5. Facials

Throw in soothing music and aromatic incense and candles and you've got yourself the guarantee of a wonderful afternoon of fantastic relaxation!

Strategy 6: Yoga

Yoga To Relax Your Mind & Body

Yoga is essentially a series of poses and stretches that when done correctly can give you relief from the stresses of everyday life. Yoga also incorporates breathing exercises that also aid in helping you to fully relax. Practitioners report that Yoga is an excellent way to relax and it helps them respond to various situations in a calmer more controlled manner. Some of the poses are more complex than others and can result in injury if done improperly, so it's always advisable to practice yoga with a qualified instructor when you are first starting out.

3 Different Types of Yoga to Try

1. **Hatha Yoga** is best if you are just starting out with yoga. It may also be called "gentle yoga" or yoga for stress relief.

2. **Satyananda Yoga** is another form of yoga that emphasizes stress relief. You can take this type of yoga if you are a beginner or if your main purpose is for stress relief.

3. **Power Yoga** is more for increased fitness than for stress relief. That doesn't mean you can't relax if you practice this form of yoga but it may be best to begin with one of the others listed above first.

Find Classes

1. Most health clubs and gyms offer yoga classes.

2. Check for ads of various instructors in your area in the newspaper and your local Craigslist online.

3. Community centers may also have yoga classes available.

Strategy 7: Hypnotherapy

The Power of Your Mind To Control Stress & Relax

Hypnotherapy has been used by millions around the world to manage the "fight or flight" response I covered earlier. The techniques used by a Hypnotherapist can help you deal with a specific problem that is contributing to your stress and control the way you respond.

For example, most people develop a set of mental, physical or emotional cues whenever they find themselves starting to stress out about something. Biting their lower lip or tapping on a table might be examples of this. Maybe they begin to perspire excessively. A professional Hypnotherapist can help you manage your stress by giving you a new physical cue to counter the stress cues.

Generally you are placed in a relaxed state of mind and given suggestions while under hypnosis. Unlike the weird stuff you see in television and movies, you are always in full control of your faculties at all times. However, in a very relaxed state of mind you can be given suggestions that are embedded subconsciously. You will remember everything but you won't consciously focus on the new suggestions.

So for instance when you find yourself beginning to feel stressed you may be given the physical cue to cross your fingers on your right hand or tap the side of your leg 3 times. During the hypnotherapy session you may be told that each time you cross your fingers or tap your leg for example you will instantly feel relaxed, stress free and ready to deal with whatever is in front of you.

It may take a few sessions before you'll begin to see results.

Finding A Hypnotherapist

1. If you know someone who has been helped by hypnotherapy ask him or her for a referral.

2. Ask your family physician

3. Search online for a Hypnotherapist in your area.

Strategy 8: Get A Hobby

Do What You Love!

When you were a young kid, you probably had lots of hobbies you enjoyed such as rock collecting, a growing doll collection, stamps etc. As we get older life gets in the way and we stop engaging in old hobbies we loved when we were younger. If you have a hobby that you've neglected just because your life got too busy, consider taking it up again or starting a new one. Just the act of spending time woodworking, sewing, quilting or collecting things can be very relaxing.

It doesn't matter really what your hobby is because the level of satisfaction and relaxation is relative to you. Your friend may find collecting coins relaxing while restoring old motorcycles may be the most relaxing activity for you.

1. Sit down and write down old hobbies you used to enjoy and then make a list of new hobbies you would love to do.

2. Then schedule time each week to do nothing but work on your hobby.

3. Make it a priority in your life and you'll really start to look forward to spending time doing something that makes you feel good.

Strategy 9: Fun Social Events

Get Out And Have Some Good Clean Fun!

Sometimes stress can be so bad that it makes you want to stay at home and be miserable. Well that's the last thing you want to do. Instead of avoiding family and friends get out of the house and have some fun. Whatever you're worried about is not going to go away just because you're hiding out at home. If you get out and spend time with those who care about you, the stress you've been feeling won't have as strong a hold on you.

Being around loved ones also reminds you that you are not alone in the world and you have people in your life ready to lend a hand. Cutting yourself off from family and friends can open the door to deep depression.

So make plans to get out regularly and laugh! Laughter is one of the best defenses to stress. It is a natural remedy to relax your mind and calm your thoughts.

Ask For Help

1. Don't let your pride keep you from asking for help. Sometimes a friend may have a simple solution to a problem that seems insurmountable.

2. Seek advice from those you trust. When you're stressed, your decision making can be a bit off, so allow a close friend to offer advice or help you come up with solutions.

3. Find places to go to lift your spirits.

4. Go to an amusement park and be a kid again!

5. Have dinner at a favorite restaurant with family and friends.

6. See a positive movie.

7. Go bowling even if you're terrible at it. All of those gutter balls will make you laugh!

8. Try something new like learning how to ballroom dance or maybe take salsa lessons.

9. If finances are tight, invite friends over for a potluck dinner and a movie.

10. Spend time at a nearby park and enjoy the scenery.

Strategy 10: Pets

There's A Reason That A Dog Is Man's Best Friend

Having a dog or cat or some other animal can do wonders for your stress level. It's quite common for nursing homes, assisted living facilities and even children's hospitals to allow animals, especially puppies and dogs to be brought into the facilities. Research has shown that dogs ease fears and help patients reduce stress.

If you have the patience, interest and time consider adding a four legged furry new friend to your life. Their personalities and loyalty can bring a lot of joy to your life and help you manage your stress. Caring for a dog who is totally dependent on you, can have a way of putting your stress in check. Plus the funny antics you'll get to enjoy with your dog will have you smiling and focusing less on negative stressful thoughts.

Tips For Choosing The Right Breed For You

1. Research different dog breeds and choose carefully based on your lifestyle, living situation (house or apt) and tolerance level. You don't want to choose a breed that may be too high strung if you're trying to tame your own stress.

2. Decide if you're prepared to get a young puppy and whether or not you have the time to properly train your dog or have the means financially to have training done by a professional dog trainer.

3. If you prefer getting an older dog consider your local animal shelter or dog rescue organizations. There are plenty of wonderful dogs that need homes.

Strategy 11: Aquariums

Fish Can Calm The Mind & Lower Your Blood Pressure

A study was done several years ago that concluded that one could manage their blood pressure and stress by simply sitting and watching fish in an aquarium. That might sound really boring but have you ever actually tried it? Before you run out and buy an aquarium, make a date to go to your local public aquarium or a local pet store. Try to go during the week when crowds are less likely to be a factor. Find a quiet spot and observe. Get as comfortable as possible and just watch.

Soon you'll begin to feel comfortable, peaceful and relaxed. It's amazingly simple but very effective in calming your mind.

Tips

1. If you've never owned an aquarium before, it would be a good idea to read a few books on setting up and caring for fish.

2. As soothing as aquariums are they do require a lot of upkeep. You'll have to keep the water clean and feed your fish on a schedule.

3. Make sure you have the right combination of fish to keep "fish fights" at a minimum. Fighting fish wouldn't be a good idea for lowering your blood pressure!

4. Cleaning the tank properly and maintaining filtration systems and such are really important to maintain healthy fish.

Although getting an aquarium requires a lot of responsibility to maintain, it can be a great way to end your day and relax your mind.

Strategy 12: Regular Massage

Weekly Massages

Strategy #5 talked about scheduling a spa day to help get rid of stress. Depending on your lifestyle that may not be possible. Instead, you might consider getting regular weekly massages. A massage therapist is trained to massage your muscles and relieve tension and stress.

When you are under a lot of stress your body carries that stress. Tight muscles and aching backs can all be the result of stress. Everyone carries stress in different places in their body. Common stress areas are the shoulders and lower back areas. They can feel like giant knots. Sometimes you may not even be aware of how much stress you're carrying until you get a massage. You can actually feel it when a massage therapist is trying to get a muscle to loosen up. Often it can take several sessions before your muscles "give in" and relax.

Tips

1. Look for licensed massage therapists.

2. Ask family and friends for referrals.

3. If cost is a factor check with your insurance plan. Some plans will pick up the tab for massage therapy or a percentage of the costs.

4. Your place of employment may also offer as part of your benefits free or discounted massage therapy.

5. Check for specials in your area at health clubs. Many clubs offer massage therapy as part of the club membership at a discounted rate.

6. There are also massage therapists who will come to your home if you prefer.

Strategy 13: Therapy And Support Groups

Therapy Can Work Wonders

Therapy and support groups can be a great way to relieve your stress. Talking about whatever is causing stress is an excellent way to work your way back to a more relaxed state of mind. Of course therapy takes time, but if you're willing to stick with it you'll learn ways to better cope with stress and manage it better as well.

Support groups can be good especially if you tend to bottle everything up inside which just creates more stress. Getting stuff off your chest can go a long way to putting you back in control of your thoughts and learning from others how to deal with certain situations better.

Therapy can also teach you how to respond to stress in ways that doesn't send your fight or flight response over the top. Once you learn new coping skills you will find yourself a lot less stressed because you will have the confidence to deal with whatever triggers your stress and rise above it.

Tips

1. Always look for a licensed therapist.

2. Your physician can often recommend a good therapist.

3. Be open minded and be willing to give it 100%.

Strategy 14: Take A Real Vacation

When You Need A Vacation From The "Vacation"!

If you really want to give yourself a real break and leave stress behind, you have to take a "real" vacation. That means not working on projects from your jobs. If you're self-employed it means not taking client projects on vacation with you.

Tips

1. Choose a vacation destination where you can truly relax. Plan to stay away from the usual touristy areas. This way you won't be drawn into constantly running around for every tour and shopping trip scheduled by trendy hotels.

2. Choose to stay where you can really do nothing but relax, read a book or just enjoy the scenery.

It may be difficult to relax the first time around because you probably have no idea what it means to really relax. Even on vacation you feel like you need to be running around doing something. Resist the urge to do that and allow yourself to relax for real and I guarantee after a couple of days you'll feel the difference.

Strategy 15: Unplug!

Disconnect!

With computers, tablets, smart phones and satellites capable of zooming in to almost any destination in the world and broadcast within minutes, it's easy to get sucked into information overload. It can add significantly to your stress.

The solution is simple although you may find it difficult to do all at once. Unplug yourself from all of your gadgets for a few hours a day. I know that seems a bit much but give it a try and see how lighter you feel. Allow yourself to just enjoy the quiet and listen to your thoughts. When we have something we're stressed about, it's easy to avoid thinking about it by focusing on other things. Too many calls, text messages, voice mails, emails and negative TV programming can add to your stress without you realizing it.

Tips

1. Try going silent for one hour once a week.

2. Add an additional day each week

3. Do this for 30 days straight. (I talk about "The 30 Day Challenge" in more detail in my book "How to Be Positive")

4. Once you get into the habit of unplugging for an hour each day you'll begin to look forward to the quiet. You'll think more clearly and find yourself more relaxed.

Get rid of the noise in your life and relax.

Strategy 16: Get Your Sleep!

Sleep - One of The Best Stress Relievers

Getting a good night of sleep can go a long way towards getting your mind to relax. If you're not getting quality sleep, you'll wake up cranky and typically have a bad day because you're tired, unable to focus and you're not as mentally sharp due to a lack of sleep.

Sleep is important for your body to function properly. Your body needs lots of rest to be ready to meet the demands of each day along with proper nutrition to provide fuel for your body to function at optimum levels.

Another reason sleep is important has to do with helping you with problems that are causing stress. Your mind takes everything you say throughout the day as well as your dominate thoughts and uses that information to sort things out. That's why you have dreams about things that happened during the day. When you use one of the strategies here before going to sleep at night, you can clear your thoughts from the stresses of the day and sleep with a relaxed mind instead. It will make a world of difference.

Tips

1. Try prayer/meditation before going to sleep.

2. Recite positive affirmations or scriptures over and over again as you drift off to sleep.

3. Give yourself an hour of no television right before bed.

4. Perform deep breathing exercises.

5. Use visualization techniques in strategy #18 to clear your mind and put yourself in a relaxed state of mind before sleep.

If you are unable to sleep and suffering from insomnia talk to your doctor and get a check-up to be sure it's not due to something serious.

Strategy 17: Diet

A Poor Diet Can Contribute To Stress

Sugar can put a lot of stress on your body. It can cause the arteries in your heart to narrow. Sugar forces your body to produce large amounts of insulin. Various organs have to work a lot harder when you eat a lot of sugar. Some research even suggests that eating foods high in sugar interferes with your ability to think clearly.

That's a lot going on inside your body. Think about how just eating bad foods could cause further stress for you mentally without you even realizing that the culprit is that delicious chocolate donut? The solution is simple. If you eat a lot of sugary foods, you've got to lay off the sweets. Besides the stress sugar puts on your bodily functions, it's also the number one reason why obesity is at an all time high in the U.S.

Tips

1. Take it one day at a time. Stopping cold turkey could have adverse effects and instead you'll find yourself pigging out twice as much on sugar laden foods.

2. Reduce your intake of sugar based foods over a 30 period. Challenge yourself and don't give up.

3. When you crave something sweet grab your toothbrush and brush your tongue. Your taste buds are on your tongue and scrubbing with toothpaste might help you to get rid of the craving for a sweet snack.

Strategy 18: Visualization

Visualize A Better Outcome

Visualization can be a powerful tool against stress. Instead of focusing on the problem itself you can use visualization to see yourself reacting in a more positive way. Seeing pleasant outcomes removes some of the stress and allows you to relax your mind and think more clearly.

The one thing that visualization techniques will not do is make your problems magically disappear. You should think of it as another form of meditation because when you are fully engaged in visualization it requires all of your senses in order to be really effective.

Tips

1. Visualize yourself handling the problem confidently.

2. Be aware of the sounds and sights in the scene. The more detailed you can be the better.

3. Spend no more than 10-15 minutes each day visualizing.

4. You will begin to notice that you're not bothered as much and your thoughts are no longer causing you as much stress.

5. Be consistent and you'll find you are better able to manage your stress and enjoy longer periods of relaxation.

Like anything else you'll get better with practice. Don't get discouraged if you suddenly find your mind drifting off to mundane things. It's natural. Just gently bring you thoughts back to your visualization. The mind needs to be trained to focus. If you are persistent you'll soon enjoy all the benefits of a relaxed mind and body.

You can find several books and information online that can teach you how to visualize effectively.

Strategy 19: Breathing Exercises

Deep Breathing

If you're like most people your normal breathing is from the chest area and you rarely consciously take deep breaths from your abdomen. Every now and then you may notice your body forces you to take a deep breath. The reason deep breathing is so beneficial for aiding in relaxation is because of the increased amount of oxygen your body gets when you breathe deeply.

Tips

1. Sit in a comfortable chair with your back straight.

2. Inhale through your nose and deeply from your abdomen.

3. Hold for a brief second and then exhale through your mouth, making sure you exhale as much air as possible.

4. As you inhale and exhale count each breathe to yourself.

5. Repeat this for 10 or 15 minutes.

This deep breathing exercise is an excellent way to combat stress. The effects are immediate and the increased oxygen will give you a nice energy boost. Also you'll find the act of counting each breathe forces your mind to focus on breathing and counting and so it has a meditative quality as well.

You can use this deep breathing exercise anytime you're feeling stressed or use it as a way to start your day.

Strategy 20: Have A Cup Of Tea

Tea To Relax Your Mind

Tea has been around for thousands of years and has been used for medicinal purposes in Asian cultures for many generations. There are several teas you can try that can be used to relax your minds and chase stress away.

1. **Passionflower tea** is used by some Native American tribes to control anxiety which leads to stress.

2. **Ashwagandha tea** which is common in India, Africa and the Mediterranean is used to help control your fight or flight stress hormones. This natural herb has a tranquilizer effect on your central nervous system. The result is you become relaxed and calm.

3. **Siberian gin-sing** is known to increase blood circulation and gives you a mental boost as well. This tea also helps to regulate stress hormones within your body.

4. **European Hawthorn tea** helps lower blood pressure in individuals with high amounts of stress hormones.

Some of the teas mentioned here are used by doctors to help patients manage their stress. In some cases, the tea is prescribed because it can be just as beneficial as a specific pharmaceutical drug. Always check with your doctor before trying any of the teas listed. Your doctor can determine whether or not it will be safe or beneficial for you to begin a tea regimen to manage your stress.

Strategy 21: Aromatherapy

Certain smells can trigger stress while others actually calm the mind and put you into a relaxed state of mind. Aromatherapy is basically the use of various plants and herbs and other ingredients called essential oils. If you've ever gone to a spa or had a massage you probably noticed pleasant smells throughout the spa and especially where the massage took place.

You don't have to go to a day spa to experience aromatherapy. You can purchase aromatherapy kits for home use almost anywhere and create your own home routine to relax after a long day or anytime you need a little extra help dissolving the stresses of the day.

Here are few of the most popular scents for relaxation.

Lavender

The smell of lavender is used to induce sleep and improve mood. Studies have shown that lavender can also reduce cortisol levels as well. It also has a positive effect in improving cognitive thinking.

Rosemary

This scent is also great for improving your mood and in the reduction of cortisol levels. While you would not want to use lavender while you're working because of it's ability to make you sleepy, rosemary does not induce sleep so if you're having a tough day and your stress level is up, Rosemary would be a good idea.

Peppermint

When you tired and stressed peppermint can help you become more alert and it's also good for memory.

Strategy 22: Count to 10

This may seem too simple to be effective but you will be surprised. When you find yourself getting stressed over something and you feel your fight or flight response ready to go into overdrive stop and slowly count to 10. This can help you in a couple of ways.

First, by removing yourself mentally and emotionally from the situation you eliminate the possibility of things escalating. Second, by counting you're giving yourself and your mind time to regroup and get yourself together. This will allow you time to calm down and clear your head so you're less likely to say something you might regret later.

Another thing you could try, would be to count backwards from 10. The reason you might try this is to tell yourself that when you reach the number one you will be calm and relaxed. It's just a way of giving your mind a mental cue to relax at one. This technique tends to work best when practiced over time.

Give each a try and use whichever works best for you.

Strategy 23: Lay Off The Caffeine

Caffeine Is Not Your Friend

This is perhaps the simplest of all the strategies listed. Too much caffeine can make your stress even worse. When you are stressed out about something, the last think you want to do, is to add the jitters and loss of sleep to the mix.

If you're not ready to give up your coffee and soft drinks, then try not to drink anything with caffeine within 4 hours of bedtime. Otherwise your sleep may be interrupted, your mood will take a nosedive and your stress will take over.

Strategy 24: Deal With The Issues That Are Stressing You Out

Finally, the final strategy is simply to deal with the issues that are causing you so much stress in the first place. It can be difficult to face up to problems, but at some point you have to if you ever want to get past it and get back to enjoying your life.

You'll find that talking about whatever it is can feel like a ton of bricks have been lifted off your shoulders. Getting it all out in the open can then open up channels to finding a solution to solve the issues instead of letting them take over your life.

Tips

1. Consider speaking with a therapist. This is a great option if you don't feel comfortable talking to family and friends. A therapist will not share what the two of you discuss and you can feel secure knowing that what you talk about with a therapist will remain between you and him or her.

2. If you are comfortable speaking with a family member or close friend then by all means do so. They may be able to offer a solution you hadn't thought of that could help you relax knowing there's a light at the end of the tunnel.

3. If you are active in a church, synagogue or temple seek advice from someone who can provide spiritual counseling to help you deal with stress.

Feeling Relaxed Can Change Your Life

Take your time and try as many of the strategies I've included here until you find some that feel right for you. You may even find combining two or three or more works best. You now have some ideas you can use right now to work toward managing your stress and learning how to relax.

These strategies have worked for thousands of people and one or more will work for you too.

Make relaxation a priority in your life and in time you'll reap the benefits of better health, a lot less stress and happier relaxed mind.

Next Steps

I really hope that reading this book has helped you to think about ideas and action steps that you can take to start realizing more success, happiness and real change in your life.

If you've enjoyed this book, I'd really appreciate it if you would take a moment to leave an honest review. I'd really love to hear from you, and I very much appreciate your comments as I love to put a name to those who are serious about creating change in their lives.

We're in this together and I want you to know that you have a cheerleader in me!

Be sure to check out my "How to Lose 100 Pounds" series if weight loss and getting healthy is part of your own personal transformation goals.

I also want to take a moment to let you know about a FREE gift I have for you.

It's a PDF report you can download called, "Your Self Development Plan: Tips for Creating Change in YOUR Life!" All you have to do is sign up for it at the site below:

ABiggerPlan.com

I'm excited for you and all the possibilities that your future holds!

To YOUR success,

Paula

Now Available in Audio

"The Personal Transformation Project" is now available as an audiobook!

You can listen to a free sample here:
Amazon.com/dp/B00JEOH4O8/

Visit the author website for additional audiobooks:

ABiggerPlan.com

Additional Titles by P. Seymour

Visit ABiggerPlan.com

****

Series "How to Lose 100 Pounds"

Creating YOUR Plan for Weight Loss Success

How to Find the Motivation to Lose Weight and Get Healthy

Goal Setting for Weight Loss

Eating for Weight Loss

Exercise for Weight Loss

Getting Back on Track After Gaining Weight

SAVE OVER 45% with the Compilation Guide!
(Includes ALL 6 Books Above)
How to Lose 100 Pounds: The Compilation Guide
*Also available in paperback

Resolutions in the New Year...or Any Time: How to Make a Plan for Transformation